Essential Music Theory © 2023 by San Marco Publications. All rights reserved.

All right reserved. No part of this book may be reproduced in any form or by electronic or mechanical means including Information storage and retrieval systems without permission in writing from the author.

ISNB: 9781896499279

Contents

Lesson 1: **Pitch and Notation**   1

Lesson 2: **Time**   7

Lesson 3: **Major Scales**   14

Review 1   20

Lesson 4: **Minor Scales**   24

Lesson 5: **Intervals**   32

Lesson 6: **History**   38

Lesson 7: **Chords**   41

Review 2   47

Lesson 8: **Naming Keys**   51

Lesson 9: **Melody**   55

Lesson 10: **Music Analysis**   61

Review 3   64

Music Terms and Signs   68

1
Pitch and Notation

Review - The Grand Staff

The treble and bass staves combine to form the ***grand staff***. This staff is used by the piano because both clefs are needed to cover its large range. The treble clef is on the top, and the bass clef is on the bottom. They are joined by a line and a brace or bracket. Figure 1.1 contains the grand staff with its notes. Middle C occurs in both clefs in the middle of the grand staff.

Figure 1.1

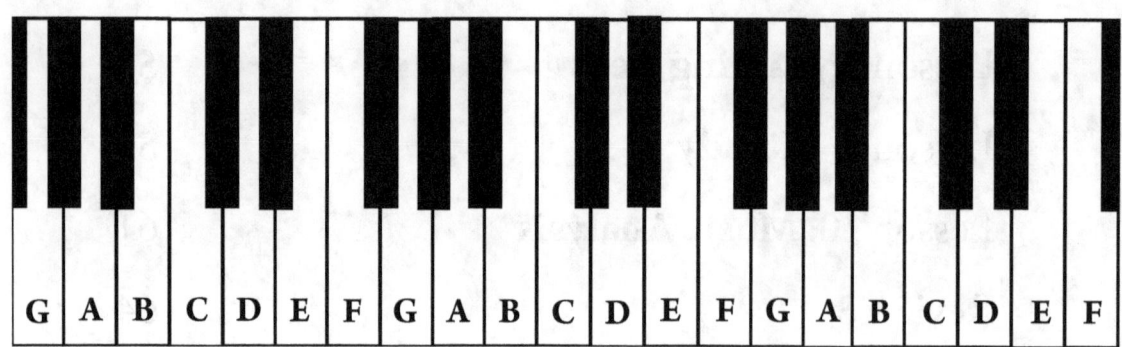

Ledger Lines - Extending the Staff

A staff has five lines and four spaces and holds nine notes. However, there are a lot more than nine notes. A staff can be extended up and down using small lines called **ledger lines**. A ledger line is a small horizontal line spaced the same distance as the lines of the staff itself. It occurs above or below, and holds the notes that are higher or lower than the staff. A ledger line is only as long as the note it is attached to, and is never used unless it is attached to a note. The alphabetical order of the musical alphabet continues as you move above or below the staff using ledger lines. In this level, we are going to study notes that are three ledger lines above and below the staff. Figure 1.2 shows the notes that are three ledger lines above and below the treble staff.

Figure 1.2

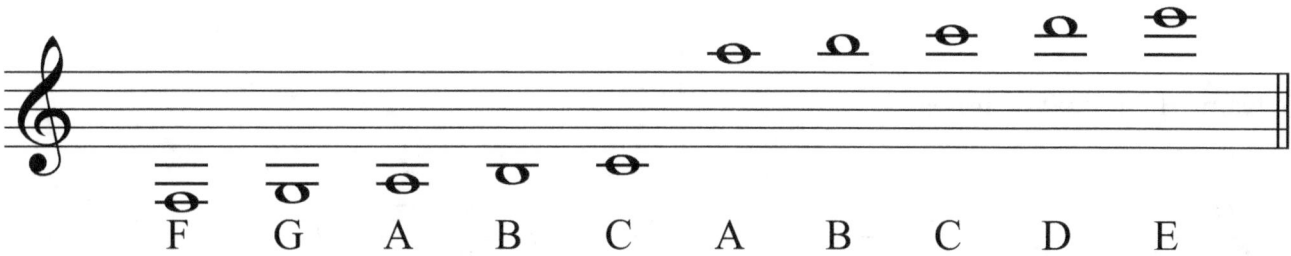

Figure 1.3 shows the notes that are three ledger lines above and below the bass staff.

Figure 1.3

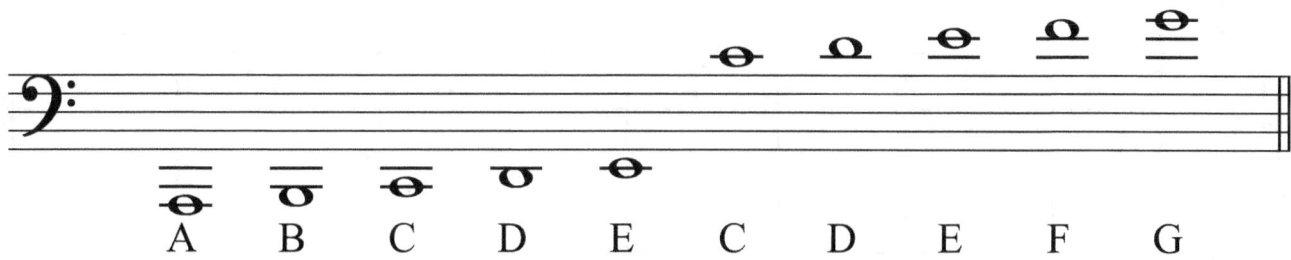

Pitch and Notation

1. Write the following note on the treble staff using ledger lines. Make no two notes the same.

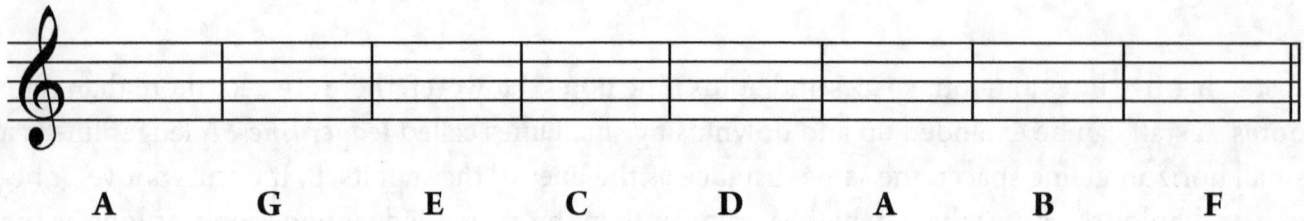

    A   G   E   C   D   A   B   F

2. Write the following note on the bass staff using ledger lines. Make no two notes the same.

  F   A   B   C   D   E   C   G

3. Name the following notes.

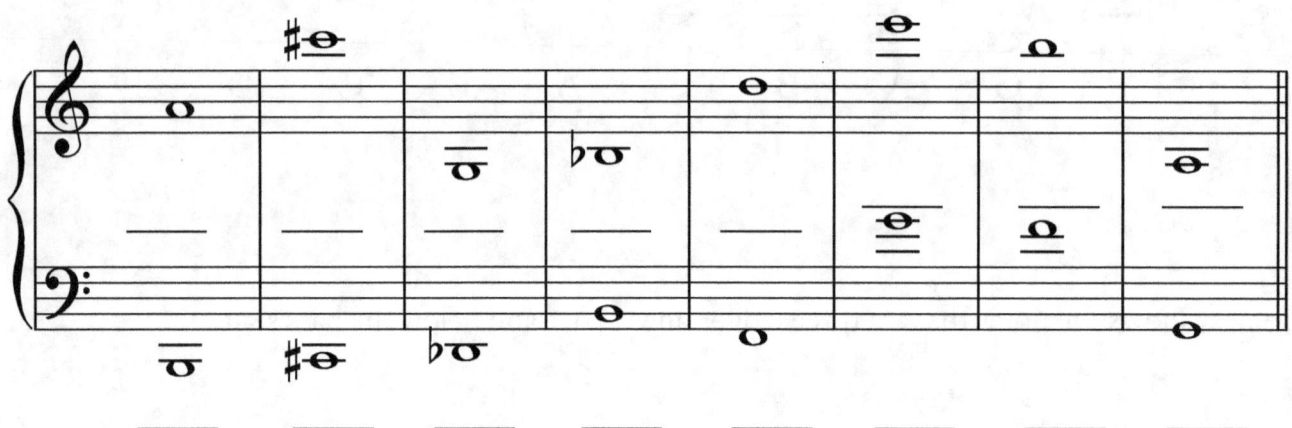

4. Write the following notes on the grand staff. Make no two notes the same

  D   F#   A   G   B♭   C   E   C#

  A   B   C   G   F   D♭   E   F#

Pitch and Notation

Stem Direction

Figure 1.4 shows the rules involving stem direction:

1. Note stems are one octave in length.
2. Stems placed on the right side of the note head extend **upward** if the note is **below the third line** of the staff.
3. If the note is **above the third line** of the staff, stems are placed on the left side of the note head and extend **downward**.
4. If the note is **on the third** (middle) line, stems **may go up or down**.
5. For eighth notes, the flag appears on the right side of the stem in all cases.

Figure 1.4

1. Add stems and flags to the following notes.

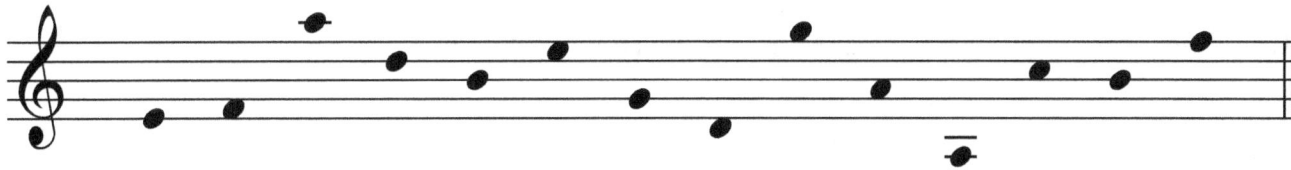

2. Circle the notes that are not correctly written.

Pitch and Notation

When we beam a group of eighth notes sometimes one or more of the stems are placed differently than would be the case if flags were used. If most of the notes are above the third (middle) line of the staff, stems go downward (Figure 1.5 a). If most of the notes are below the third line, the stems go upward (Figure 1.5 b). Here, majority rules.

Figure 1.5   a)   b)

If the number of notes above the middle line of the staff is equal to the number below, the stem direction is determined by the note which is the farthest from the middle line (Figure 1.6).

Figure 1.6

1. Connect each group of four eighth notes with stems and beams.

Music Terms - Dynamics

Dynamics is the term we use for how loud or soft we play. The two most important words to remember in reference to dynamics are **piano** (soft) and **forte** (loud). Most dynamic signs are related to these two terms. Study Figure 1.7 which is a chart of dynamic markings.

Figure 1.7

ITALIAN TERM	ABBREVIATION	MEANING
pianissimo	*pp*	very soft
piano	*p*	soft
mezzo piano	*mp*	medium soft
mezzo forte	*mf*	medium loud
fortissimo	*ff*	very loud
forte	*f*	loud

2
Time

Time Signatures

Level 1 covered 2/4, 3/4 and 4/4 time. **C** is an abbreviation for 4/4 time. These time signatures have a specific pattern of strong and weak beats. Figure 2.1 shows the strong and weak beats in each time signature.

Figure 2.1

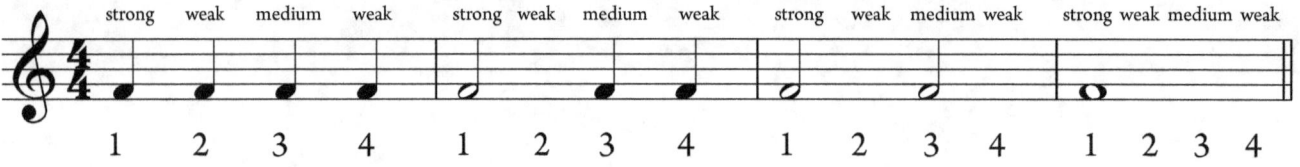

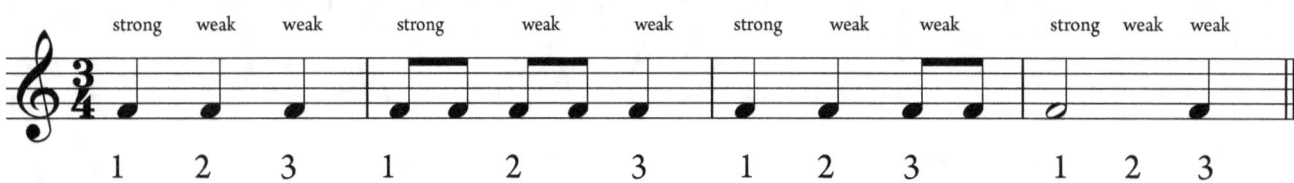

1. Add the correct time signature at the beginning of each line. Label the accents as strong (S), weak (W), or medium (M).

2. Add bar lines to complete the following according to the time signatures.

Dotted Notes

A dot to the right of a note makes it last longer. A dot adds half the value to a note. In this level, we will study dotted half and quarter notes.

The Dotted Half Note

A half note gets 2 beats. The dot is worth half of that. Half of 2 is 1 (2 + 1 = 3). This gives us a total of three. A **dotted half note** gets three beats. Figure 2.2 contains a dotted half note.

Figure 2.2

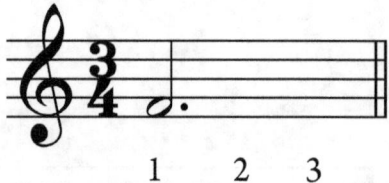

When drawing a dot beside a note in a space, the dot should be placed in the same space as the note. For a line note, the dot is placed in the space above the line note.
Figure 2.3 shows a dotted space and dotted line note.

Figure 2.3

The Dotted Quarter Note

A quarter note gets one beat. The dot is worth half of that. Half of 1 is ½ (1 + ½ = 1½). This is a total of one and a half. A **dotted quarter note** gets one and a half beats. When counting the dotted quarter it is easier to think of it as equal to three eighth notes. It helps to divide each beat using the word *and* to represent the eighth notes.

Figure 2.4

1. Add bar lines to complete the following according to the time signatures.

2. In the empty measure write **one** note that is equal to the following groups of notes.

Rest Review

Silence in music is as important as sound. A *rest* is used to show silence in music. Figure 2.5 shows the rests covered in Level 1. The whole rest is equal to one complete measure of rest. In 4/4 time it's value is 4 beats, in 3/4 time it is worth 3 beats, in 2/4 time it is worth 2 beats. This rest is used to represent one complete measure of silence no matter what the time signature.

Figure 2.5

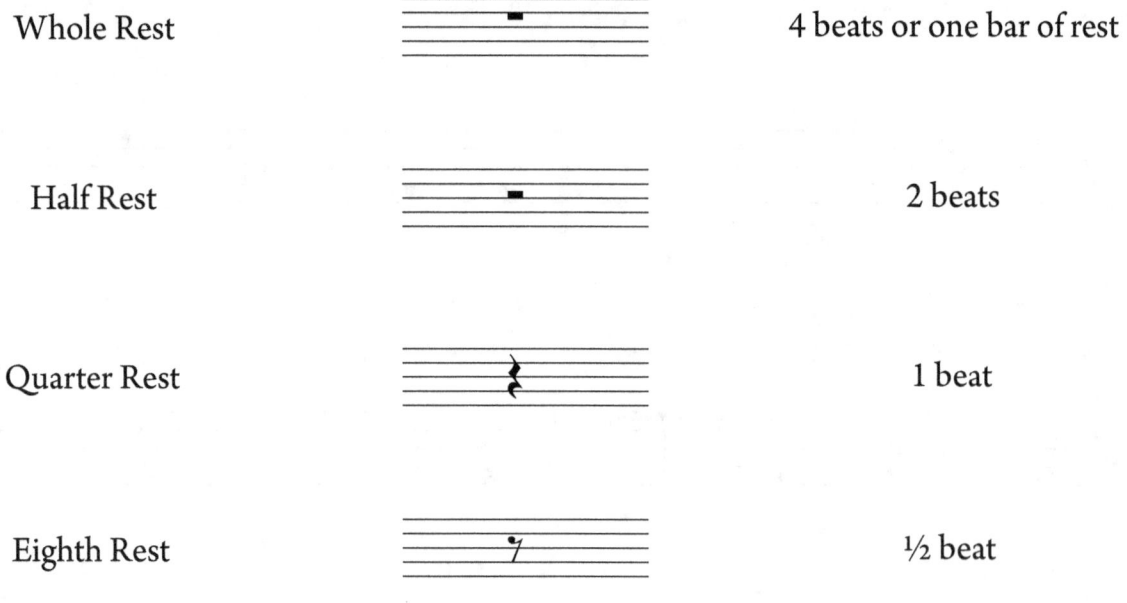

Time

1. Add **one** rest to complete each measure according to the time signature.

2. Add **one** note to complete each measure according to the time signature.

Music Signs

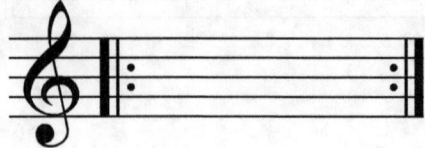

repeat marks - at the second sign go back to the first sign and repeat the music from there. The first sign is left out if the music is repeated from the beginning.

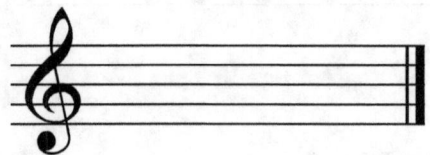

double barline - indicates the end of a piece of music.

tenuto mark - when placed over or under a note, hold it for its full value.

fermata - pause, hold note or rest longer than its written value.

pedal symbol - press/release the right pedal.

3
Major Scales

Review - What is a major scale?

A ***major scale*** is a group of notes that follow a specific order of whole and half steps. Major scales have seven pitches or eight notes with the repeated octave. We can label each note of the scale with a number with a caret on top ($\hat{1}$). This refers to ***scale degree***. The first note is scale degree $\hat{1}$, the second note is scale degree $\hat{2}$, etc. Scale degree $\hat{1}$ is the most important and is a called the ***tonic***. Scale degree $\hat{5}$ is called the ***dominant***. Scale degree $\hat{4}$ is called the ***subdominant***. Scale degree $\hat{7}$ is called the ***leading tone*** since it often leads to the tonic. Major scales are built on the following pattern of whole steps and half steps:

whole step - whole step - half step - whole step - whole step - whole step - half step

The major scale can be divided into two four note sections called ***tetrachords*** as shown in Figure 3.1. Each tetrachord is WWH with a W between them (WWH W WWH).

Figure 3.1

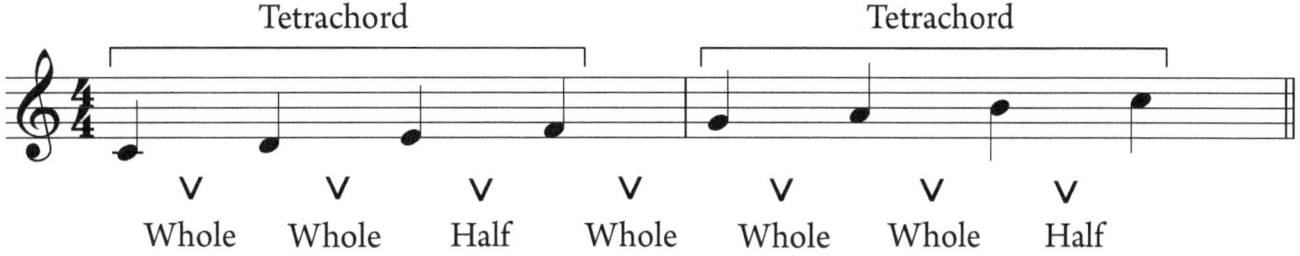

Figure 3.2 shows the major scales studied in Level 1. The key signatures are written for each scale. Major scales may be labeled as F major, C major, etc. Each scale degree is marked with a number and a sign on top called a caret ($\hat{1}$, $\hat{2}$, etc.).

Figure 3.2

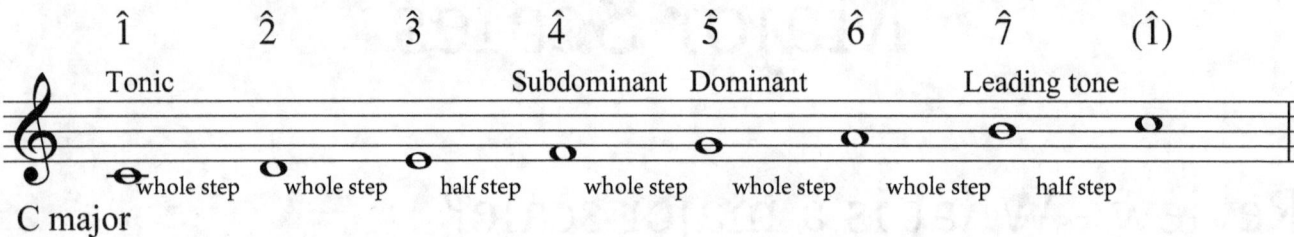

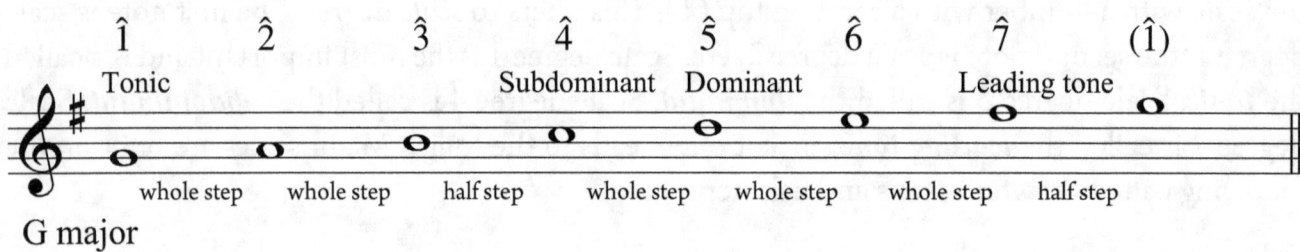

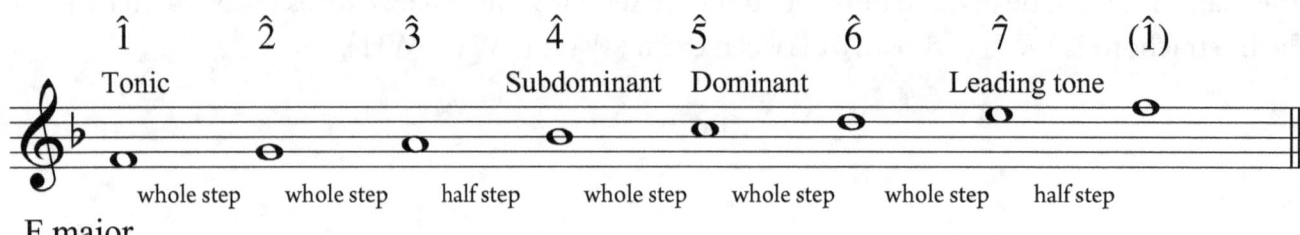

1. Write the following scales ascending and descending using a key signature. Write the scale degrees ($\hat{1}$, $\hat{2}$, etc.) above the notes. Label the subdominant (SD), and leading tones (LT) notes.

F major in whole notes

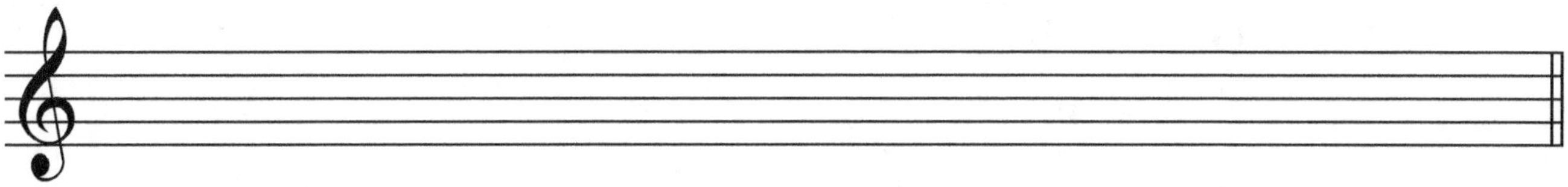

C major in half notes

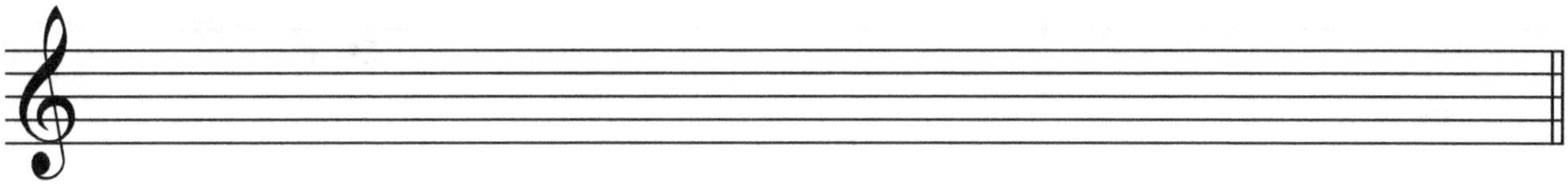

G major in quarter notes

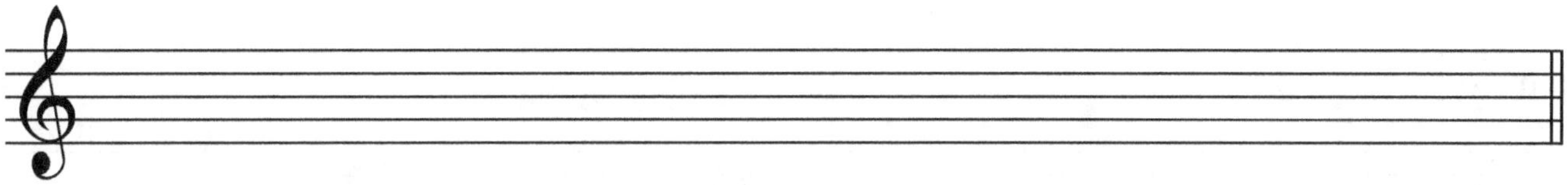

2. Write the following scales ascending and descending using accidentals instead of a key signature. Label the tonic (T), and dominant (D) notes.

C major in dotted quarter notes

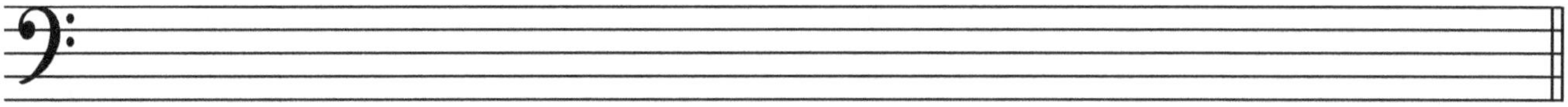

G major in whole notes

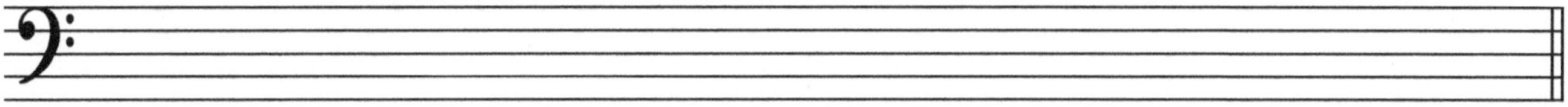

F major in dotted half notes

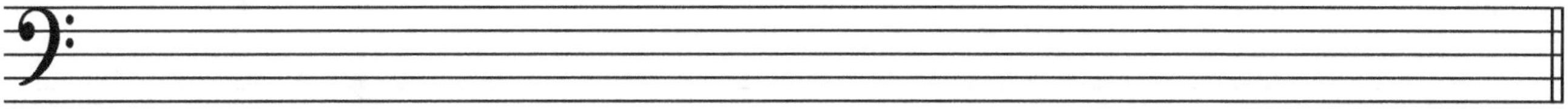

Major Scales

3. Add clefs and accidentals where necessary to create the following major scales.

C major

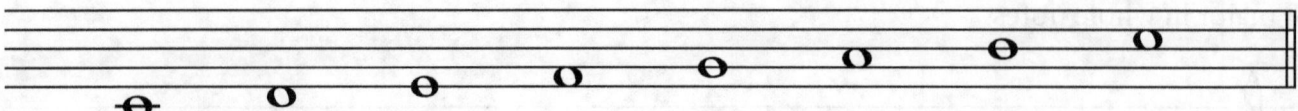

G major

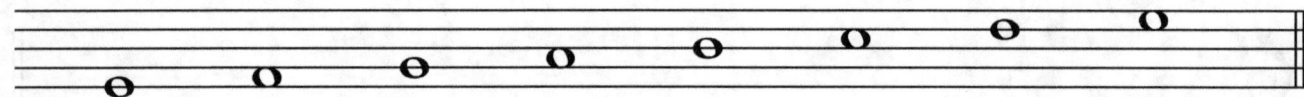

F major

F major

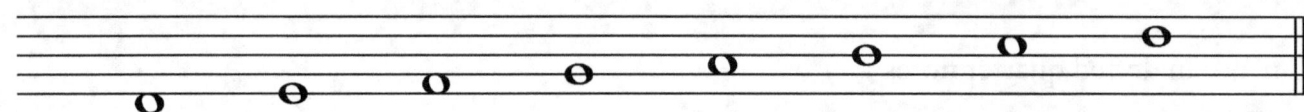

C major

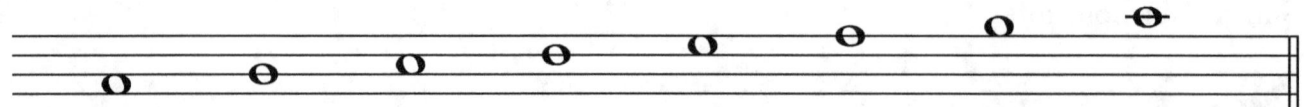

G major

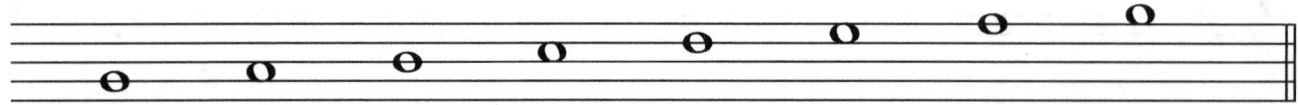

4. Name the scale degree ($\hat{1}$, $\hat{2}$, $\hat{3}$, etc.) of the notes marked with * in each of the following. The first answer is shown.

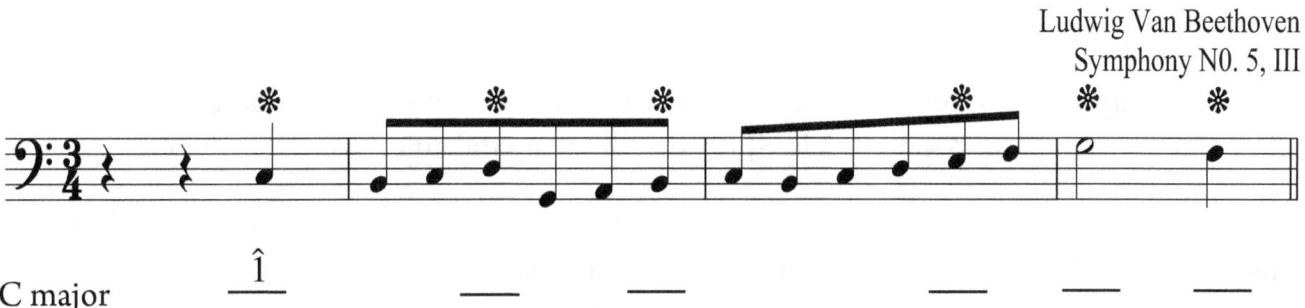

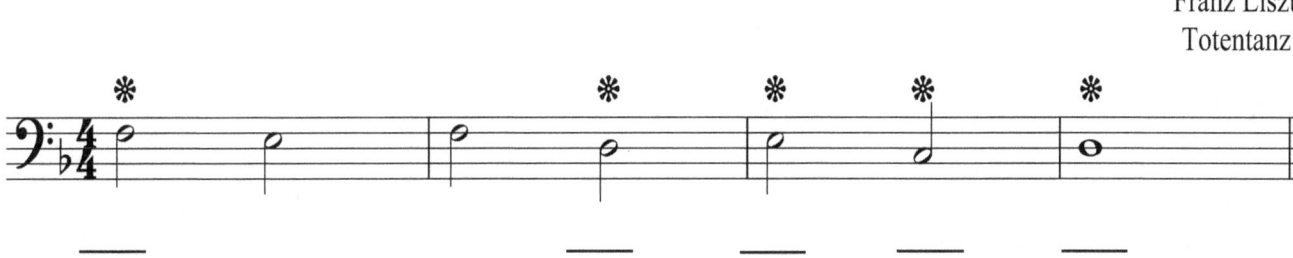

Music Terms

Terms Relating to Tempo

The word **tempo** comes from the Latin *tempus* which means time. Words that deal with tempo refer to how fast or slow we play music. Study the following Italian terms.

a tempo	return to the previous tempo
allegretto	fairly fast, a little slower than allegro
presto	very fast
rallentando, rall.	slowing down

Tempo Terms Review

5. The following terms are from Level 1. Draw lines to match the correct term with its meaning.

tempo	slowing down gradually
lento	fast
andante	at a moderate tempo
moderato	moderaltely slow; at a walking pace
allegro	slow
ritardando, rit	speed at which music is performed

Major Scales

Review 1

1. Name the following notes.

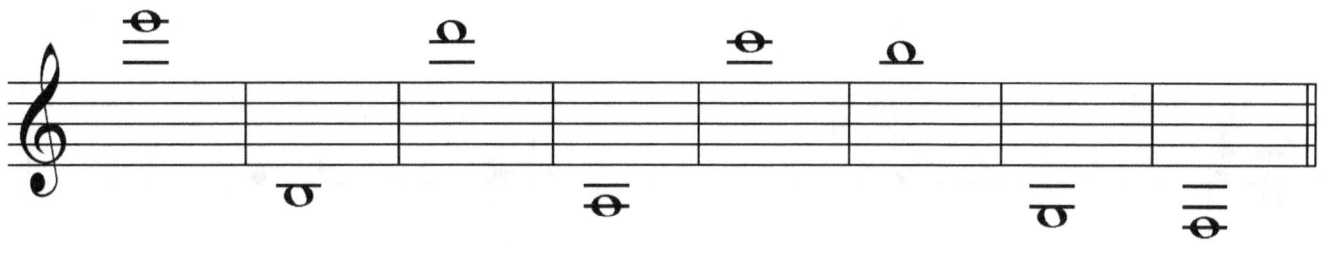

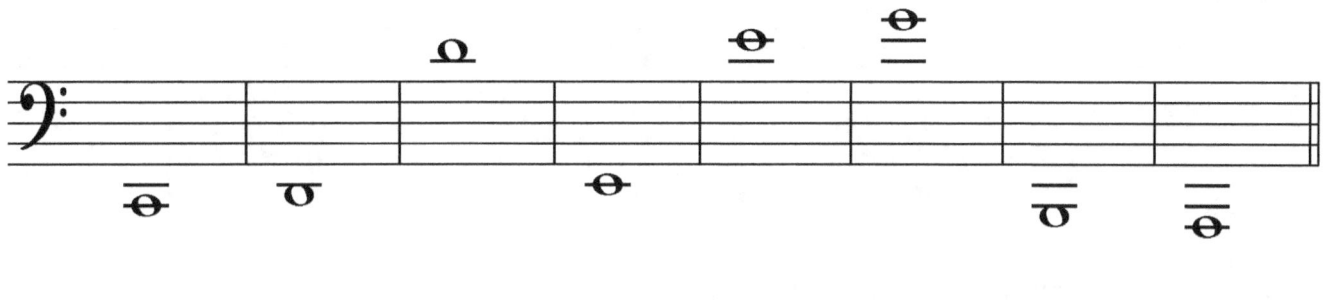

2. Write the following notes using ledger lines. Make no two notes the same.

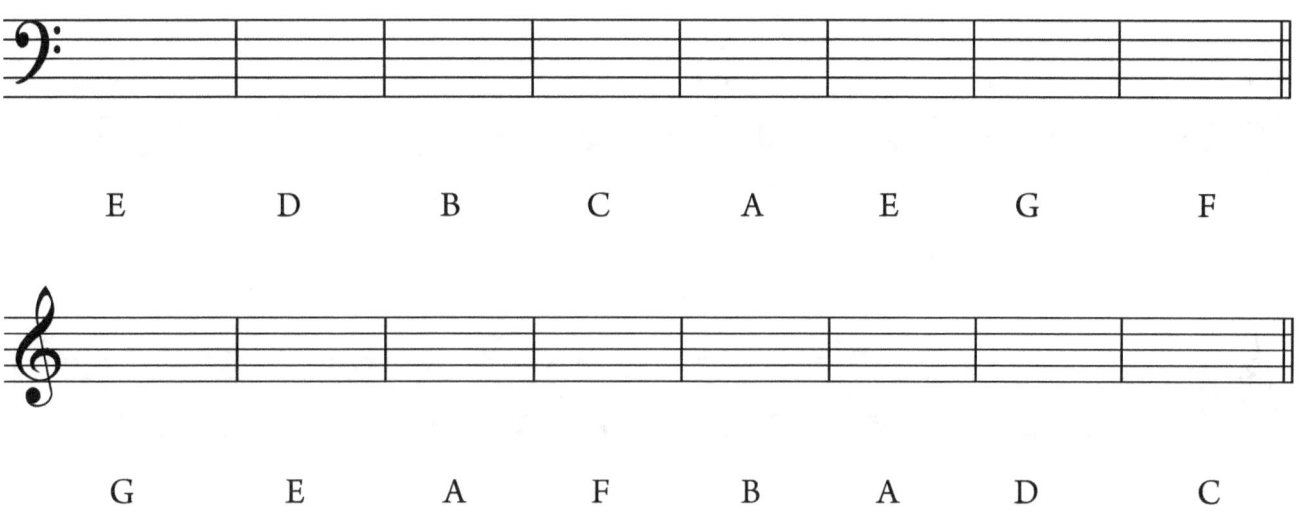

3. Add **one** rest to complete each measure according to the time signature.

4. Add bar lines according to the given time signatures.

5. Write the following major scales ascending and descending in whole notes using a key signature. Label the subdominant notes (SD).

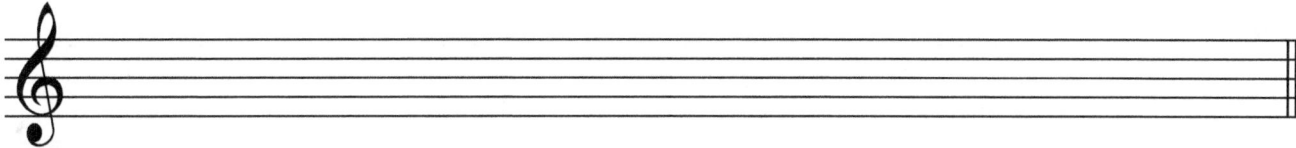

C major

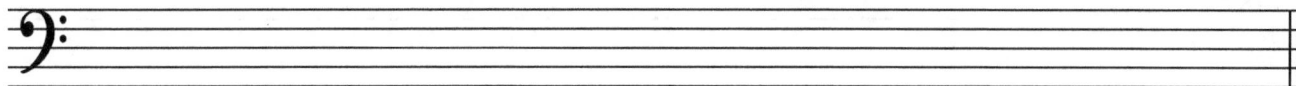

F major

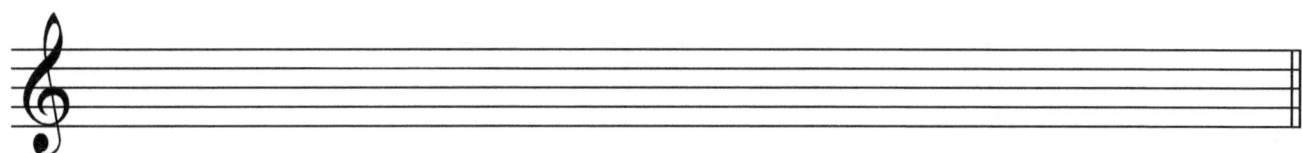

G major

6. Draw lines matching the following musical signs with their names.

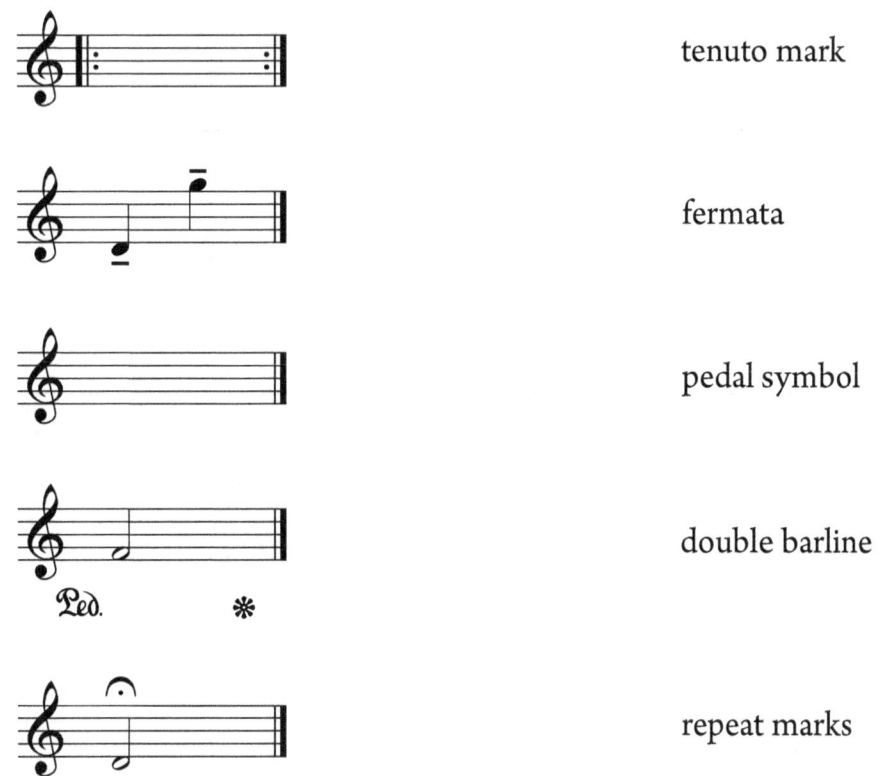

tenuto mark

fermata

pedal symbol

double barline

repeat marks

Review 1

7. Define the following musical terms.

tempo _____

lento _____

moderato _____

rallentando, rall. _____

a tempo _____

allegretto _____

andante _____

presto _____

allegro _____

ritardando, rit _____

4

Minor Scales

The Natural Minor Scale

A major scale evokes a particular color or character in sound. A ***minor scale*** has a different color or character. Some might say it has a sadder or darker sound, but that is a matter of opinion. The minor scale is another essential scale in music, and it occurs frequently.

There are three types of minor scales. We will begin by studying the ***natural minor scale***. The natural minor scale has a specific pattern of whole and half steps. This scale is constructed using the pattern WHWWHWW. The half steps occur between $\hat{2}$ and $\hat{3}$ and $\hat{5}$ and $\hat{6}$. Figure 4.1 contains the A natural minor scale, using this interval pattern. Using this pattern you can construct a natural minor scale on any note. The key is written as 'A minor.'

Figure 4.1

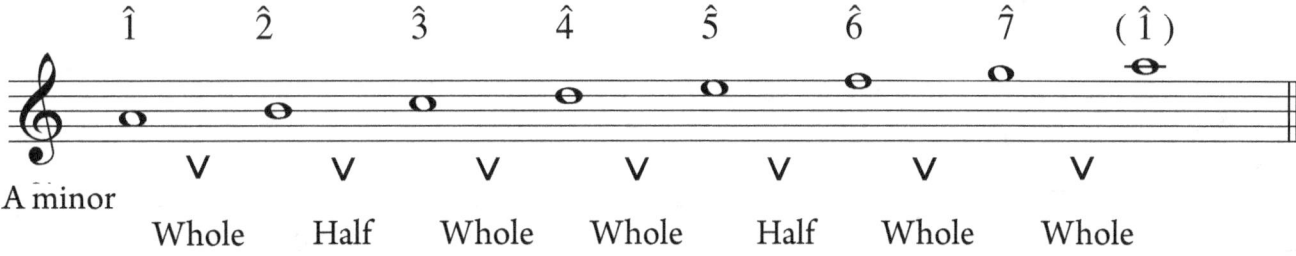

The Origin of the Minor Scale

Major and minor scales are known as **modes**. A mode is an ancient scale. If you play a major scale starting and ending on a different note than the tonic you get a mode. In fact, a minor scale lives inside a major scale. The minor scale can be found by playing the major scale from the 6th note to the 6th note.

Relative Minor Keys

Figure 4.2 is the C major scale. It is C major because of the arrangement of whole and half steps and because it starts and ends on C. C is the tonic, which is the most important note in any key. A composition in C major is all about C, and is usually centered around the note C. The tonic is home base and a piece of music sounds complete when it ends on the tonic.

Figure 4.2

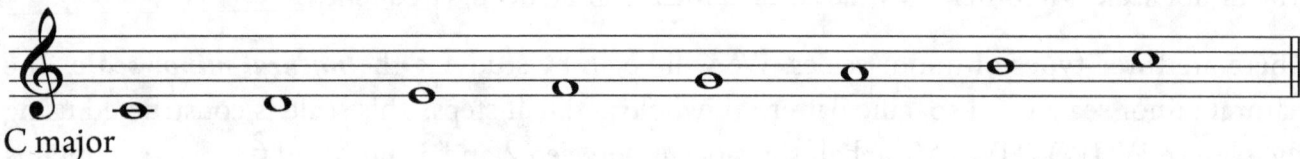

C major

If you play a major scale from the 6th note to the 6th note you get a natural minor scale. The C major scale played from A to A, produces the A natural minor scale (Figure 4.3). All of the notes in A natural minor come from the C major scale. A minor is the **relative minor** of C major. A minor and C major are related by key signature. They each have the same number of flats or sharps. C major's relative minor is A minor, and A minor's relative major is C major. Both keys have no sharps or flats in their key signature.

Figure 4.3

A natural minor

If you play the G major scale from its 6th note (E to E), you get its relative minor, E natural minor. Figure 4.4 shows these two scales using accidentals. They can also be written with the key signature of one sharp (F♯). They are related because they each have an F♯ in their key signatures.

Figure 4.4

G major

E natural minor

Figure 4.5 contains the F major scale and its relative minor, D minor. The 6th note of F major is D. These examples use the key signature (B♭). The key signature is the same for both scales because they are relatives.

Figure 4.5

F major

D natural minor

1. Name the relative minors of the following major keys.

   C major _____

   G major _____

   F major _____

2. Write the following scales ascending and descending using a key signature.
   Mark the tonic (T) and the subdominant notes (SD).

E natural minor in half notes

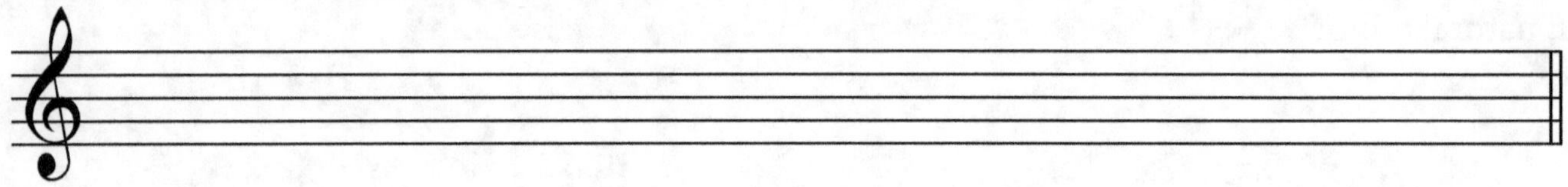

D natural minor in whole notes

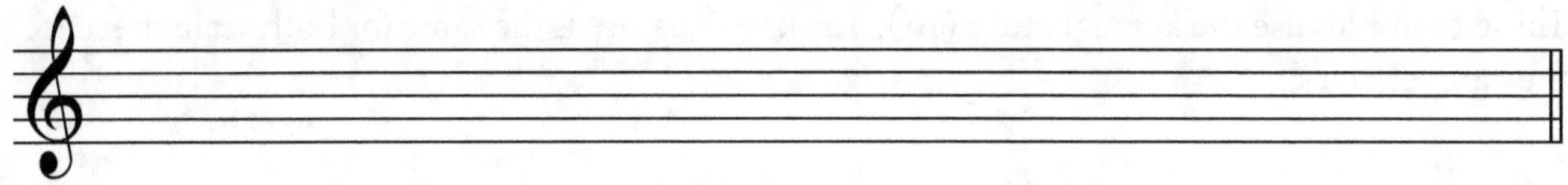

A natural minor in quarter notes

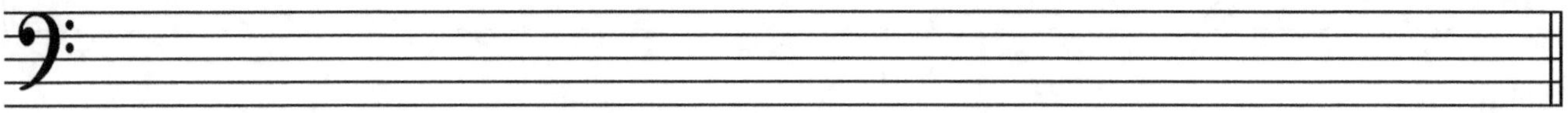

E natural minor in dotted quarter notes

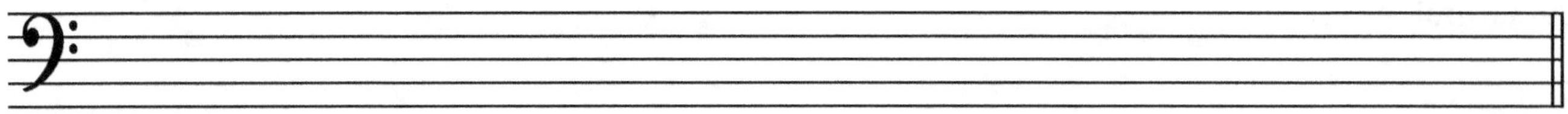

Minor Scales

The Harmonic Minor Scale

The **harmonic minor scale** is the most common minor scale. It is a slightly altered version of the natural minor scale. In the harmonic minor scale, $\hat{7}$ is raised one half step. The name harmonic comes from the way the scale is used. This version of the scale is required to get the music correct when writing chords. A half step is needed between $\hat{7}$ and $\hat{8}$ to create certain chord progressions in music. When $\hat{7}$ is a half step away from the tonic ($\hat{8}$), it is called the **leading tone** because it leads our ear to the tonic.

In the natural minor scale where $\hat{7}$ is not raised, and is a whole step away from the tonic, it is called the **subtonic**. When $\hat{7}$ is a whole step away it does not sound like it is leading to the tonic, so it is not called the leading tone. In minor keys we have two names for $\hat{7}$. When it is raised, it is called the **leading tone**. When it is not raised it is called the **subtonic**.

The harmonic minor uses the same key signature as the natural minor (the relative major), but there is an accidental for raised $\hat{7}$. Figure 4.6 contains the A natural minor scale and the A harmonic minor scale. A minor's relative major is C major so there are no sharps or flats in the key signature. The harmonic minor is simply the natural minor with $\hat{7}$ raised one half step. $\hat{7}$ is G and we use a sharp to raise it one half step to G♯. In the harmonic minor scale there are three half steps. They occur between $\hat{2}$ and $\hat{3}$, $\hat{5}$ and $\hat{6}$ and $\hat{7}$ and $\hat{8}$.

Figure 4.6

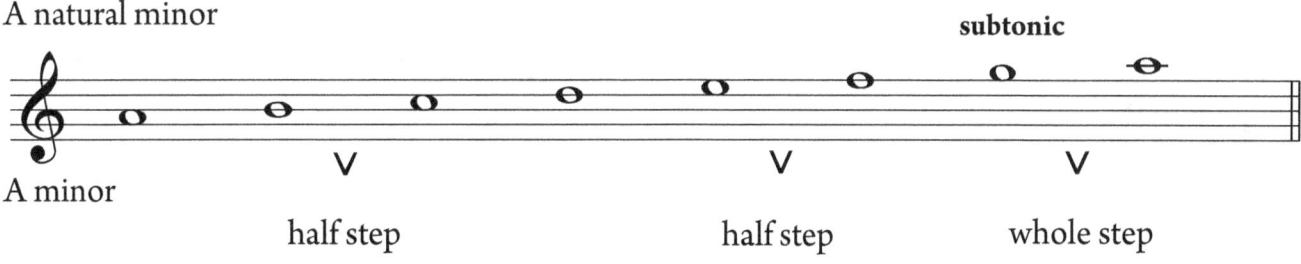

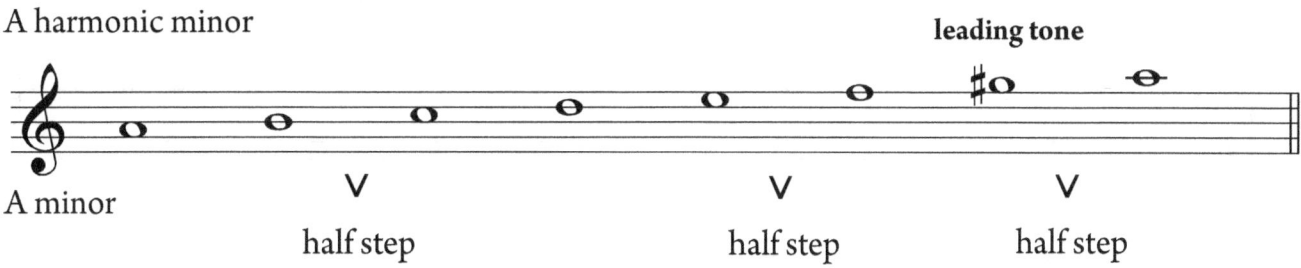

The E harmonic minor scale uses the same key signature as its relative major, G major, and raised $\hat{7}$ is D♯. In Figure 4.7, for demonstration purposes, the D♯ is written ascending and descending but this is not necessary since the D remains sharp within the same measure.

Figure 4.7

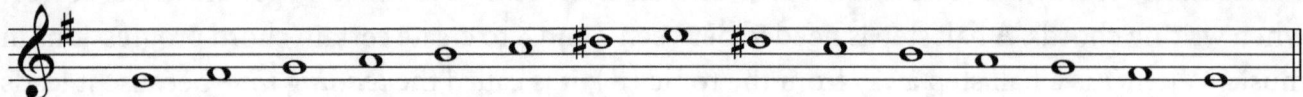

E harmonic minor

The D harmonic minor scale uses the same key signature as its relative major, F major, and includes raised $\hat{7}$, C♯.

Figure 4.8

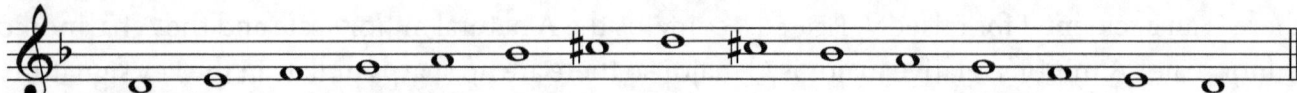

D harmonic minor

1. Using the correct key signature write the following harmonic minor scales in whole notes. Write them in both clefs on the grand staves. The first one has been started for you.

A harmonic minor

D harmonic minor

Minor Scales

2. Add clefs and accidentals to create the following scales. Label the tonic (T), subtonic (ST) and leading tones (LT).

A harmonic minor

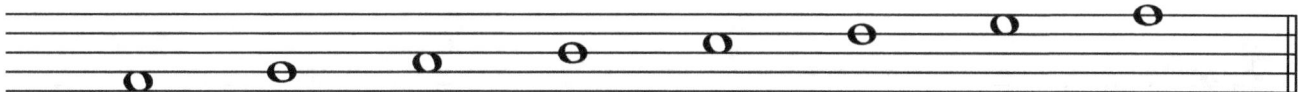

E natural minor

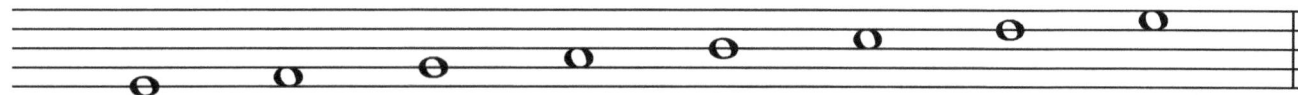

D natural minor

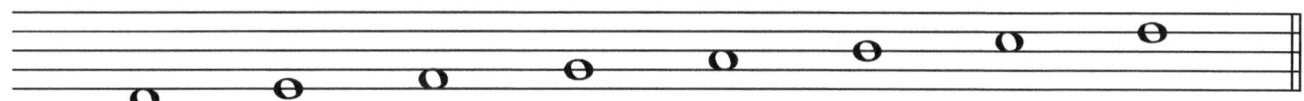

E harmonic minor

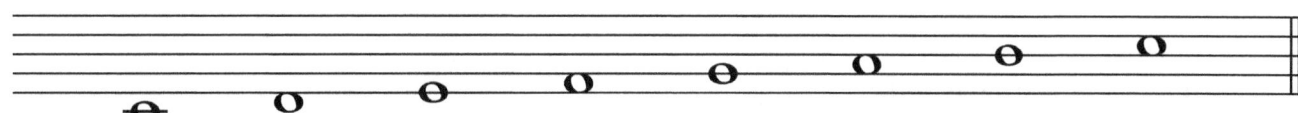

D harmonic minor

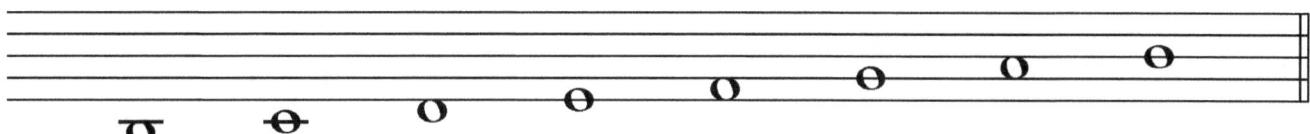

3. Using the given rhythms, write the minor scales as named below.

E minor harmonic ascending

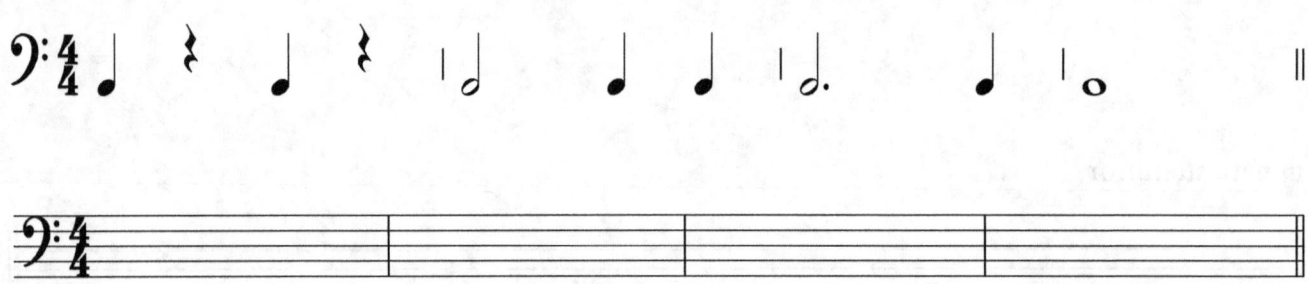

A minor harmonic decending

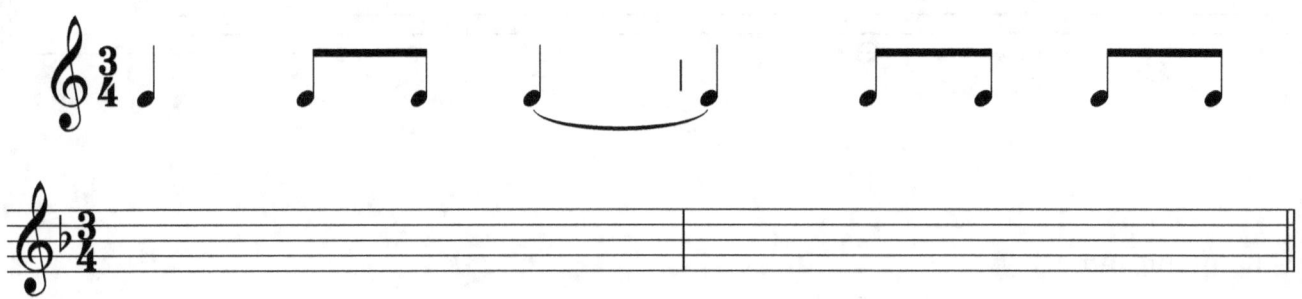

D minor harmonic asecending

5
Intervals

Half Steps

An *interval* can be defined as the distance from one note to the next. The smallest interval in the music we are studying is a **half step**. Half steps may occur between two notes using the same letter name as shown in Figure 5.1.

Study how sharps, flats, and naturals can raise or lower a note without changing its letter name.

Figure 5.1

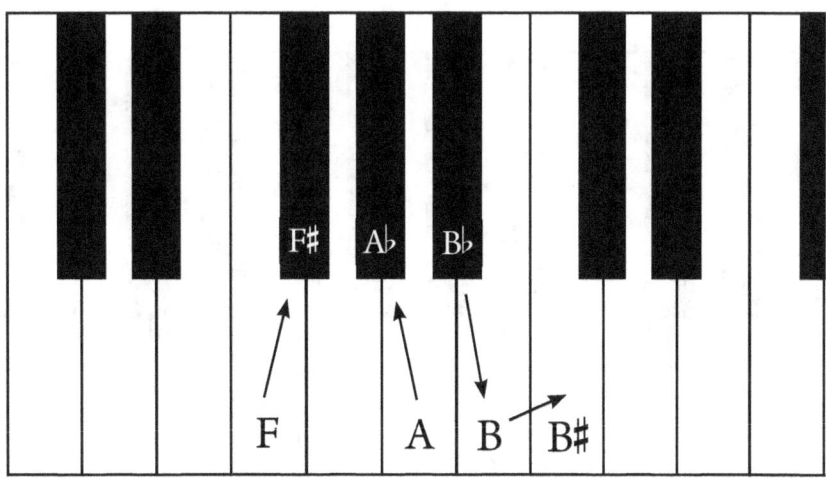

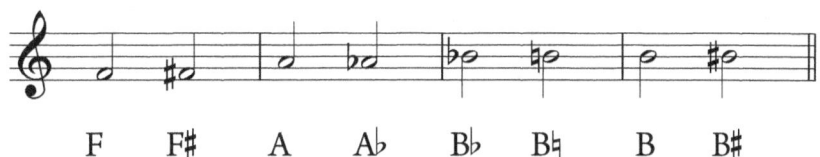

Intervals

1. Write half steps above the following notes. Use notes with the same letter name.

2. Write half steps below the following notes. Use notes with the same letter name.

Half steps can also occur between two notes with different letter names. Figure 5.2 shows half steps between notes using different letter names. The note names occur in alphabetical order. For example, E♭ - F♭, F♯ - G, A - B♭, etc.

Figure 5.2

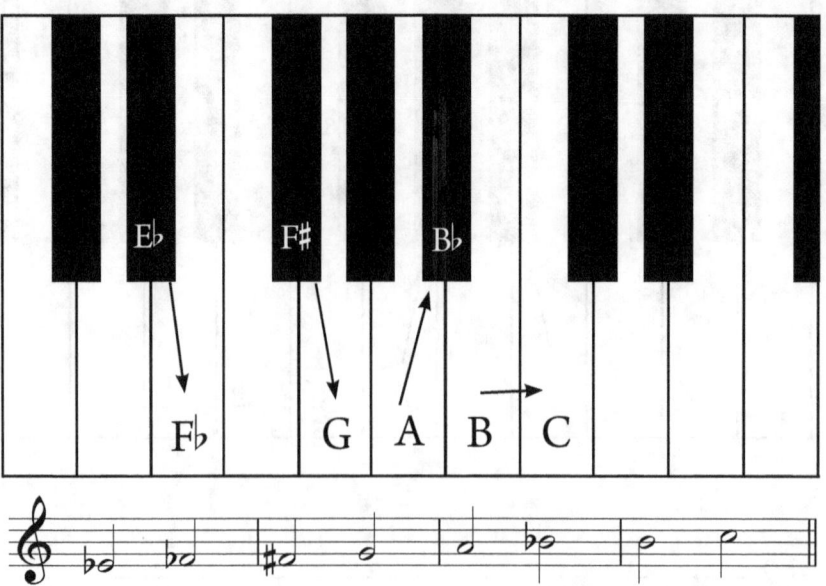

Intervals

1. Write half steps above the following notes. Use notes with the different letter names.

2. Write half steps below the following notes. Use notes with the different letter names.

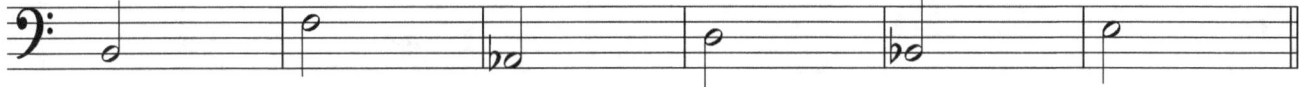

Whole Steps

A *whole step* is made up of two half steps. On the keyboard, there is always one key in the middle of a whole step. Sometimes the key is black, and sometimes it is white. Figure 5.3 shows whole steps written on the score and where they occur on the keyboard. A whole step always contains two different letter names in alphabetical order. For example, F - G, A♭ - B♭, C♯ - D♯, or if it's a whole step below, D - C, B♭ - A♭, etc.

Figure 5.3

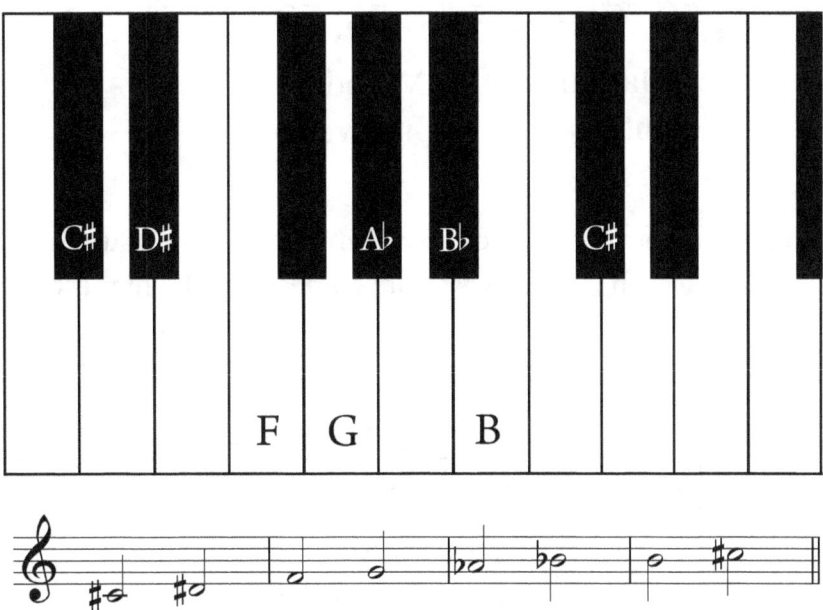

Intervals

1. Write whole steps above the following notes.

2. Write whole steps below the following notes.

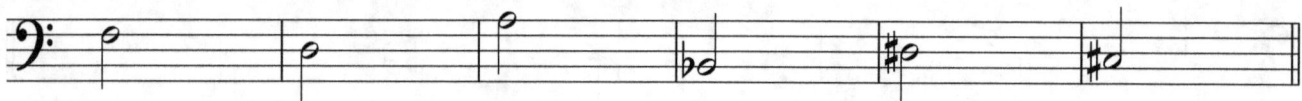

Numerical Intervals

Intervals larger than a half step are expressed as numbers. For now, we will deal with the intervals from 1 to 8. There are two basic types of intervals, **harmonic** and **melodic**.

- A harmonic interval occurs when two notes are played or sung at the same time.
- A melodic interval occurs when two notes are played or sung one after the other.

Figure 5.4

Harmonic   Melodic
Interval   Interval

Intervals are numbered. To determine the number of an interval, count up from the lowest note to the highest note. This is done even if the lowest note comes after the highest note.

Figure 5.5

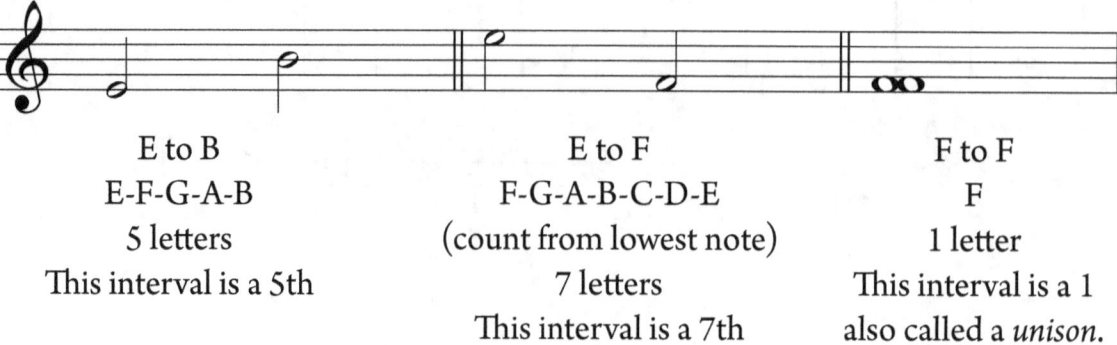

E to B　　　　　　　　E to F　　　　　　　　F to F
E-F-G-A-B　　　　　F-G-A-B-C-D-E　　　　　F
5 letters　　　　　(count from lowest note)　　1 letter
This interval is a 5th　　　7 letters　　　This interval is a 1
　　　　　　　　This interval is a 7th　　also called a *unison*.

Intervals

1. Write the following harmonic intervals above the given notes

2. Write the following melodic intervals below the given notes.

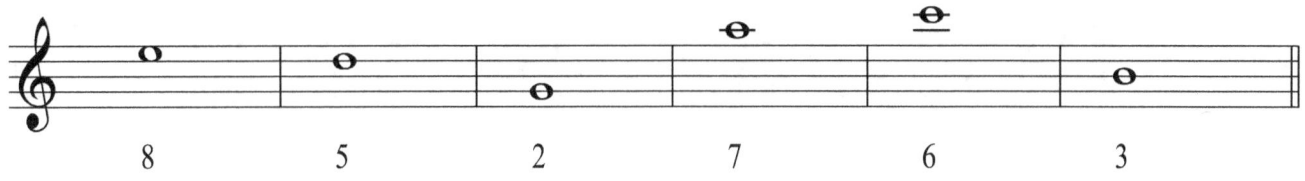
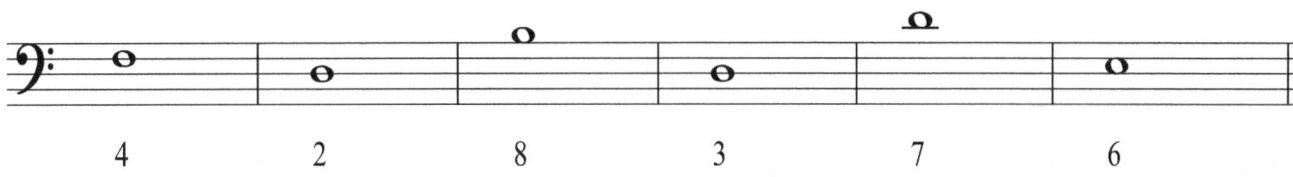

Intervals

3. Name the following intervals.

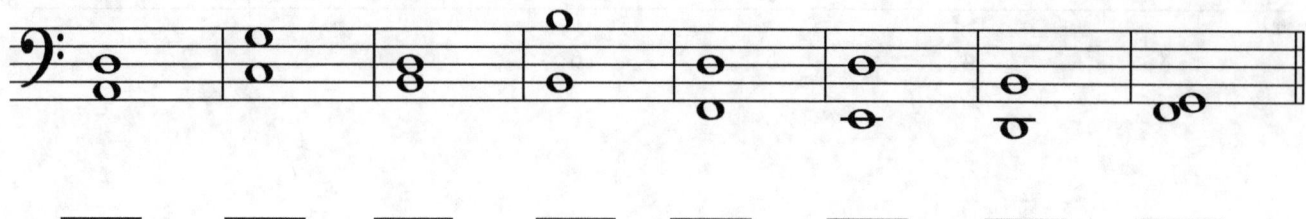

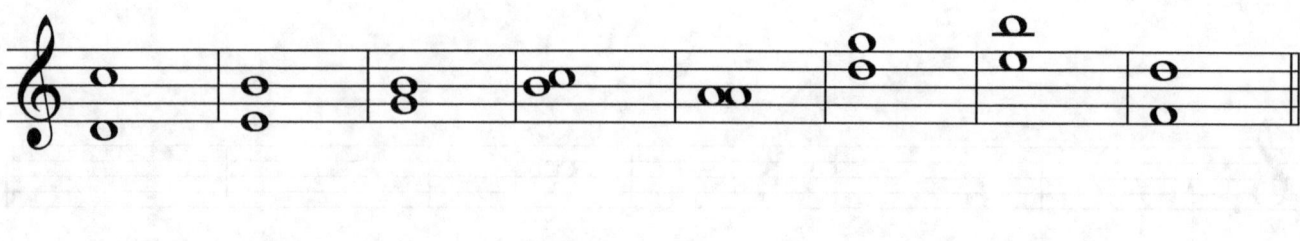

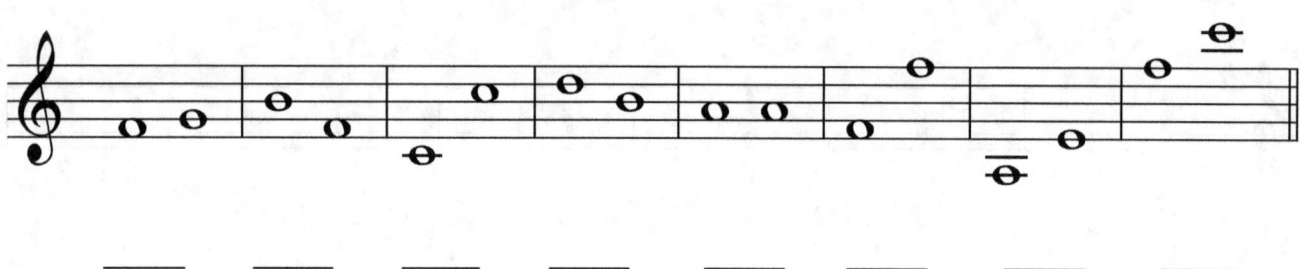

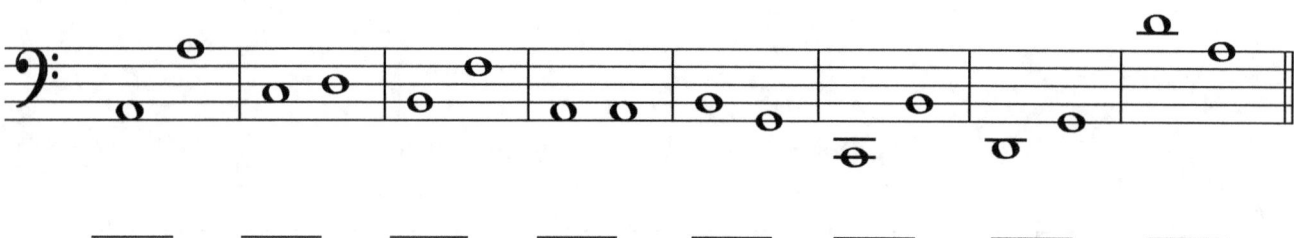

Intervals

6
History

Wolfgang Amadeus Mozart (1756 - 1791) Classical Era

Wolfgang Amadeus Mozart composed music in the ***classical era.*** The classical era was a period in history between the years 1730 and 1820. Mozart was born in Salzburg, Austria, where his father and teacher Leopold was a violinist and composer. Wolfgang was a child prodigy. He composed his first piece of music at age five, had his first piece published when he was seven, and he wrote his first opera when he was twelve. By the time Mozart was 6, he was a first-rate pianist and violinist. He and his sister Maria Anna (known as Nannerl) traveled all over Europe performing for royalty.

As an adult, Mozart moved to Vienna, to work as a pianist and composer. Mozart, no longer a child prodigy, was still a musical genius, but people no longer made a big fuss over him. At that time, musicians were treated like servants, but Mozart could never and would never think of himself as a servant.

Mozart was only 35 when he died. During his short life, he composed in all different musical forms, including operas, symphonies, concertos, masses, and chamber music. Today, he is still considered one of the greatest composers of all time!

Catalogue Numbers for Mozart's Compositions

Many composers assigned numbers to their compositions. This helped to identify them. If a composer wrote four Sonatas in C major, it was easier to identify them if they were numbered. Mozart, however, never numbered his works.

In 1862, a Viennese botanist and teacher named Ludwig von Köchel, published a catalogue of Mozart's compositions in chronological order. He assigned Köchel (K) numbers to each of Mozarts works according to the date of composition. For example, the Horn Concerto we are going to study is labeled K495. It is approximately the 495th piece of music that Mozart composed.

Horn Concerto No. 4 in E flat Major, K 495

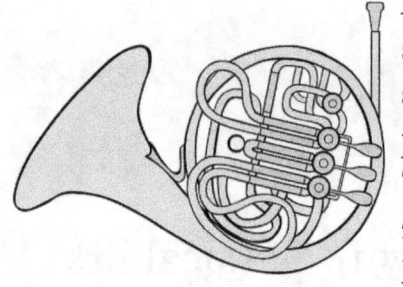

A *concerto* is a musical composition which features a single solo instrumentalist with an orchestral accompaniment. It shows off the skills of the soloist and the musical potential of the instrument being played.

This concerto is for french horn and orchestra. It was written my Mozart in 1786 for his friend, French horn player, Joseph Leutgeb.

Mozart wrote it in four colors of ink, black, red, blue, and green as a joke for his friend Joseph. Mozart had a great sense of humor.

This concerto has four sections called *movements*.

The last movement is a *Rondo*. It features a melody which is a hunting theme, which returns over and over throughout the piece. Rondos always have a section that returns many times over. Between this section are new sections consisting of different melodies or themes and musical ideas. After each new idea the original theme returns. Find and listen to a recording of this Rondo on the internet.

Twelve Variations on "Ah vous dirai-je, Maman"

Twelve Variations on "Ah vous dirai-je, Maman" K. 265, is a piano composition by Mozart, composed when he was about 25 years old (1781 or 1782). In music, variations are pieces that are based on a tune, known as the theme. This form is often called Theme and Variations. This piece consists of twelve variations on the French folk song "Ah! vous dirai-je, Maman". This well-known melody first appeared in 1761, and has been used for many children's songs, such as "Twinkle Twinkle Little Star," "Baa, Baa, Black Sheep," and the "Alphabet Song."

Mozart's Variations are composed for solo piano and consist of 13 sections; the first section is the theme, the other sections are Variations 1 to 12.

The variations were first published in Vienna in 1785.

1. Choose the correct answer.

a. Mozart was born in:	☐ France	☐ Germany
	☐ Poland	☐ Austria

b. Mozart's first teacher was:	☐ His father	☐ His mother
	☐ His sister	☐ Haydn

c. What era did Mozart live?	☐ modern	☐ classical
	☐ romantic	☐ baroque

d. What is the solo instrument in Mozart's Horn concerto?	☐ flute	☐ piano
	☐ french horn	☐ oboe

e. Mozart's Horn Concerto in E♭ has 4 sections called:	☐ groups	☐ movements
	☐ pieces	☐ dances

f. The last movement of Mozart's Horn Concerto in E♭ is a:	☐ rondo	☐ waltz
	☐ sonata	☐ minuet

g. Mozart's Variations on Ah vous dirai-je, Maman are written for:	☐ guitar	☐ orchestra
	☐ piano	☐ horn

h. How many variations did Mozart write on Ah vous dirai-je Maman?	☐ 12	☐ 9
	☐ 6	☐ 32

i. The melody upon which variations are based is called the:	☐ subject	☐ phrase
	☐ tune	☐ theme

j. The melody of these variations has been used for these childrens songs:	☐ Twinkle Twinkle	☐ Baa Baa Black Sheep
	☐ Alphabet Song	☐ Mary Had a Little Lamb

7

Chords

Chord Review

A ***chord*** is three or more notes sounded at the same time. A ***triad*** is a three note chord. The ***tonic triad*** of any key is the triad built on $\hat{1}$ of the scale or the tonic. Figure 7.1 is the tonic triad in C major. The note that the triad is built on is called the ***root***. The next note a third above it is called the ***third***. The note a fifth above the root is called the ***fifth***.

Figure 7.1

fifth
third
root

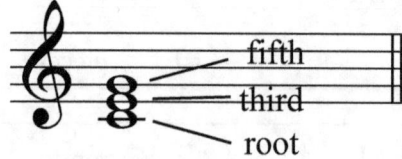

A triad can be written and played ***solid*** or ***broken***. A triad is solid when all the notes are played together or at the same time as in Figure 7.2. Another word for solid is ***blocked***. A triad is broken when the notes are played one after the other as in Figure 7.3.

Figure 7.2

Solid

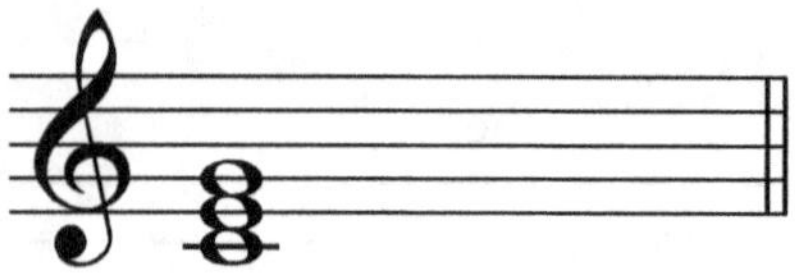

Figure 7.3

Broken

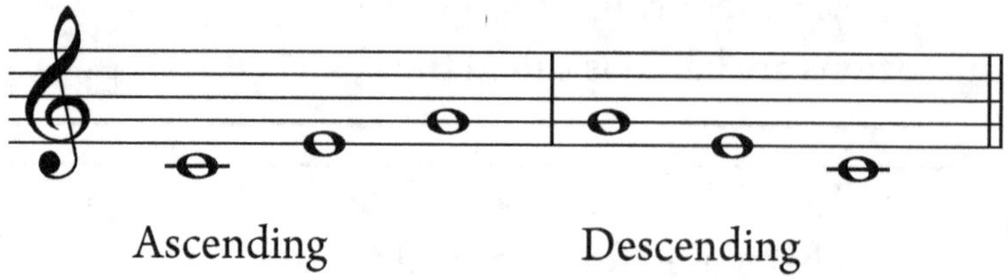

Ascending
Descending

Tonic Triads in Major and Minor Keys

A triad can be built on the tonic of a major scale by stacking thirds on the first note. This results in a ***major triad***. A triad built on the tonic of any major scale is a major triad. Figure 7.4 shows the G major triad, which is built on the tonic of the G major scale. We classify triads with figures called ***chord symbols***. There are two types shown here. One is the ***root/quality chord symbol*** which occurs above the triad. Since this is a G major triad the root/quality symbol is an upper case G. The other symbol occurs below the triad and is the upper case Roman numeral I. This indicates that this is the triad built on scale degree 1̂ of the key. We are in the key of G major here and the triad is built on G. This is called a ***functional chord symbol***.

Figure 7.4

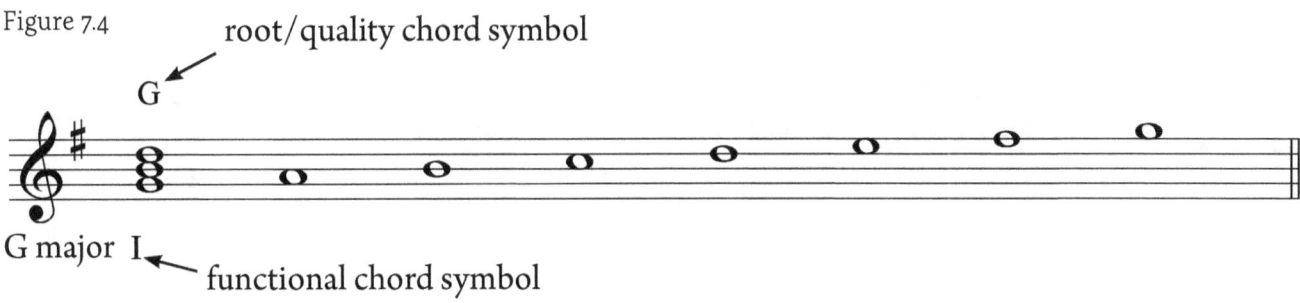

A triad built on the tonic of a minor scale results is a ***minor triad.*** Any triad built on the tonic of a minor scale is a minor triad. Figure 7.5 shows the E minor triad built on the tonic of the E natural minor scale. The root/quality chord symbol for a minor triad is the letter name plus the letter m. In this case **Em**. Some books will use the symbol Emin. The functional chord symbol is a lowercase Roman numeral **i**. This indicates that it is built on scale degree 1̂ of E minor. The lowercase 'i' means that the chord is minor.

Figure 7.5

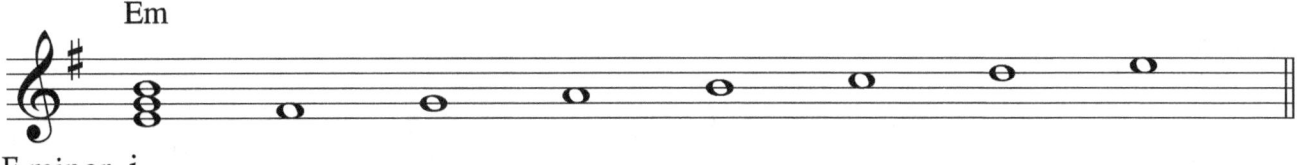

Figure 7.6 shows solid (blocked) triads built on the tonic notes of three major keys with their key signatures and chord symbols.

Figure 7.6

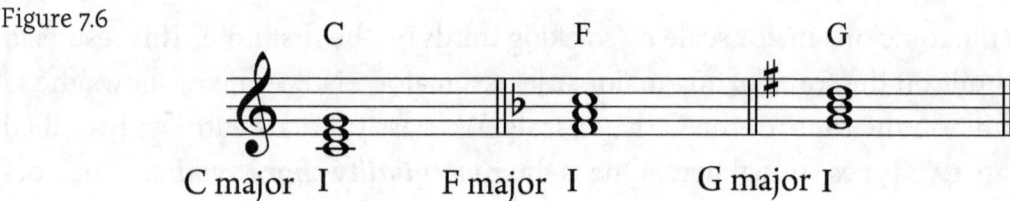

Figure 7.7 shows broken triads built on the tonics of three major keys with their key signatures and chord symbols. Broken triads may ascend or descend.

Figure 7.7

Figure 7.8 shows solid triads built on the tonics of three minor keys with their key signatures and chord symbols.

Figure 7.8

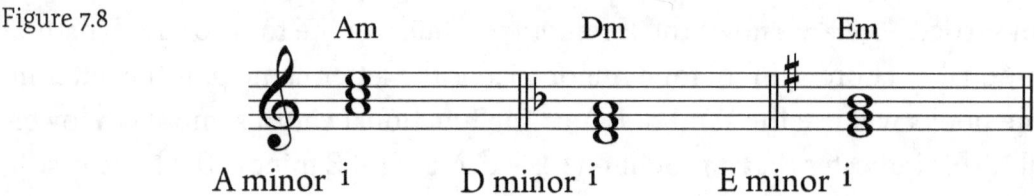

Figure 7.9 shows broken triads built on the tonics of three minor keys with their key signatures and chord symbols.

Figure 7.9

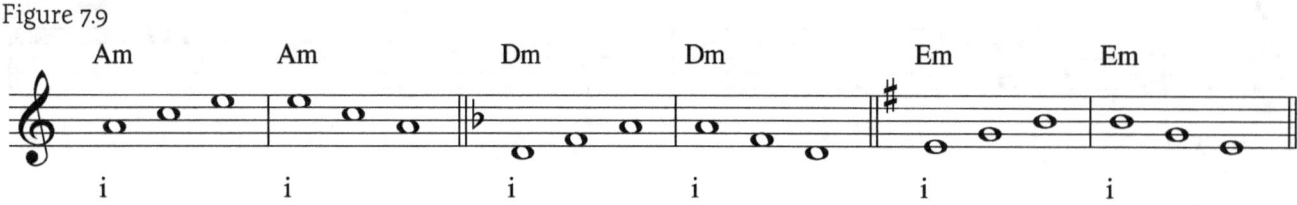

1. The following are all tonic triads. Name the key. Write the root/quality and functional chord symbol for each.

2. Write tonic triads in the following keys in solid form. Use a key signature for each. Add the root/quality and functional chord symbols.

   A minor   G major   D minor   C major   F major   E minor

   E minor   C major   A minor   F major   D minor   G major

Chords

3. Write the following tonic triads in broken form according to the root/quality and functional chord symbols. Use key signatures for each.

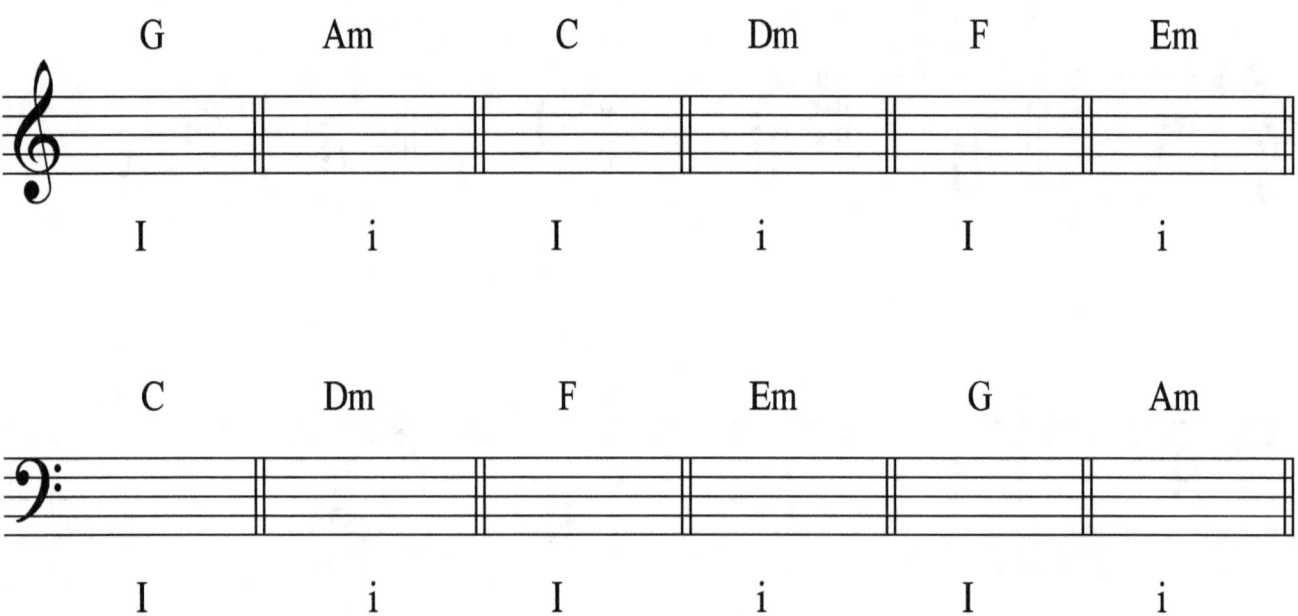

4. For the following descending broken triads: Name the key. Write the root/quality chord symbol. Name the root, 3rd and 5th of each.

key: _____	key: _____	key: _____
root: _____	root: _____	root: _____
3rd: _____	3rd: _____	3rd: _____
5th: _____	5th: _____	5th: _____

key: _____	key: _____	key: _____
root: _____	root: _____	root: _____
3rd: _____	3rd: _____	3rd: _____
5th: _____	5th: _____	5th: _____

Chords

Music Terms

Study the following music terms.

poco	little
molto	much, very
fine	the end
da capo, D.C.	from the beginning
D.C. al fine	repeat from the beginning and end at *fine*.

Review 2

1. Name the relative majors of the following minor keys.

   A minor _____

   D minor _____

   E minor _____

2. Write the following harmonic minor scales, ascending and descending, using a key signature Mark the leading tones (LT).

   E harmonic minor in whole notes

   D harmonic minor in half notes

   A harmonic minor in dotted quarter notes

3. Name the following intervals as half step (H) or whole step (W).

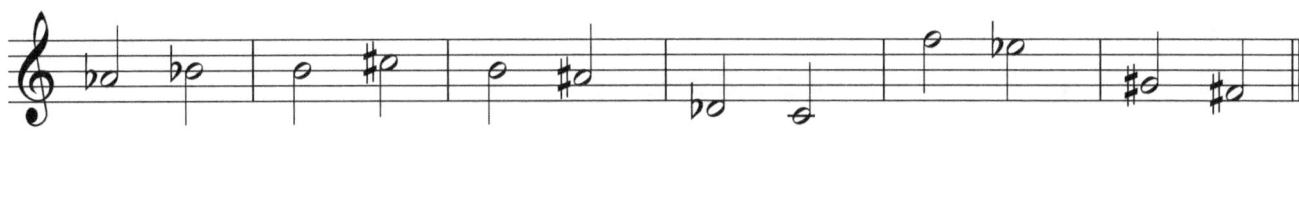

4. Give the number name of the following intervals.

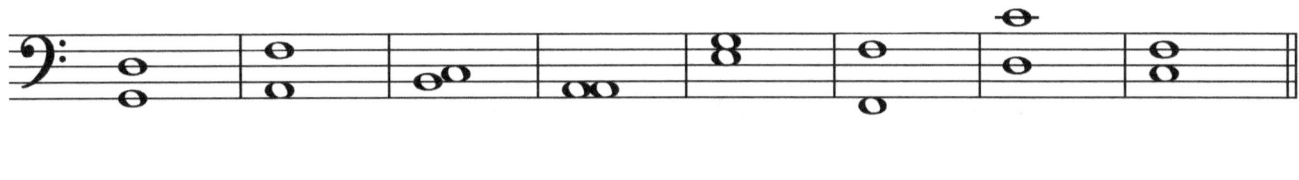

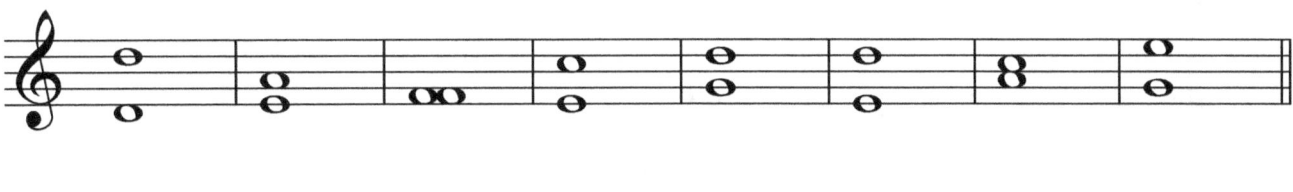

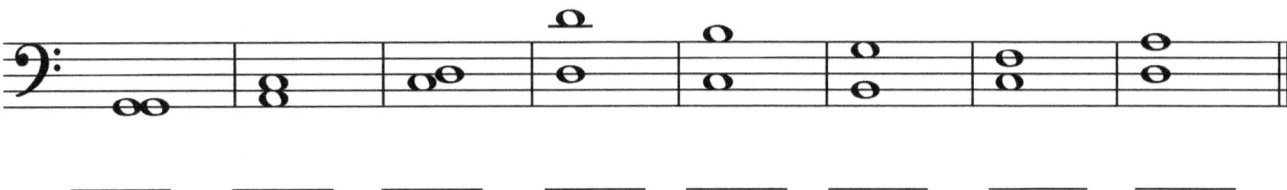

5. The following are all tonic triads. Name the key. Write the root/quality and functional chord symbol for each.

6. Write tonic triads in the following keys in ascending broken form. Use a key signature for each. Add the root/quality and functional chord symbols.

    D minor   G major   A minor   E minor   F major   C major

7. Draw lines to match the following terms with their meaning.

poco	from the beginning
molto	repeat from the beginning and end at fine
fine	little
da capo, D.C.	the end
D.C. al fine	much very

8. Answer the following questions.

a. In what country was Mozart born? _____

b. Name one instrument Mozart played. _____

c. How old was Mozart when he wrote his first opera?

      ❏ 5   ❏ 12   ❏ 7

d. Who was Mozart's first teacher? _____

e. What is the solo instrument in Mozarts horn concerto? _____

f. For which instument are the variations "Ah vous dirai-je, Maman" written? _____

g. How many variations are there in "Ah vous dirai-je, Maman?" _____

h. Name one popular childrens song based on this theme. _____

50

Review 2

8
Naming Keys

Much of the music we hear and play today is based on a specific major or minor scale. This music uses the accidentals (sharps and flats) that are found in that scale. For example, music based on the G major scale is said to be in the key of G major and uses the notes from the G major scale. The scale of G major has one F sharp. A piece in the key of G major will have an F sharp.

Figure 8.1 contains a melody in G major using accidentals instead of a key signature. This melody begins and ends with G and contains F sharps. It is based on the notes of the G major scale and is in the key of G major.

Figure 8.1

G major

The most important note in any key is the first note, scale degree $\hat{1}$. This note is called the tonic. The tonic is the central note in any key, and all other notes revolve around it. In fact, pieces often, but not always, begin and end on the tonic. The tonic is the home base for a key, and this is why it is effective at the beginning and end of a piece. It establishes the key. It is very strong to start and end at home (the tonic).

The melody in Figure 8.2 is in the key of C major. Notice how many times the tonic (C) appears in this melody.

Figure 8.2

C major

To determine the key of a melody it is important to look at the key signature first. A key signature suggests two keys: the major key and its relative minor. For example, a key signature with no sharps or flats could suggest the key of C major or A minor. Most minor keys will have accidentals indicating raised $\hat{7}$. This raised note is an important part of the minor key and is usually present in minor melodies. If there are G♯'s in the melody, it may be in the key of A minor.

The melody in Figure 8.3 has a key signature of one flat. This indicates the key of F major, or its relative minor, D minor. There are no raised notes indicating D minor. D minor should have raised $\hat{7}$ (C♯). In this melody the C's are natural. The first and last note is F, another strong indication of F major. This melody is in F major.

Figure 8.3

Wolfgang Amadeus Mozart
Minuet in F

F major

Figure 8.4 has a key signature of one flat, indicating F major or D minor. The melody has a C♯ which is raised $\hat{7}$ of D minor. It begins and ends on a D. This melody is in D minor.

Figure 8.4

Henry Purcell
Air

D minor

1. Name the keys of the following melodies.

key: _____

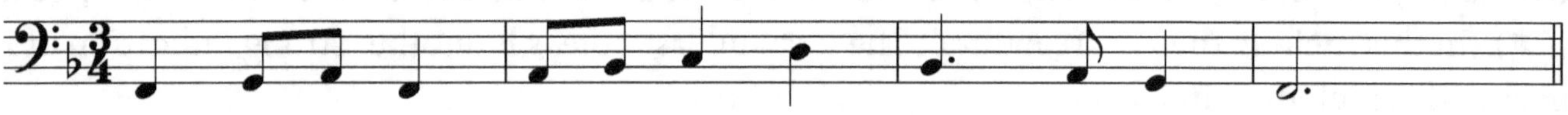

key: _____

key: _____

key: _____

key: _____

key: _____

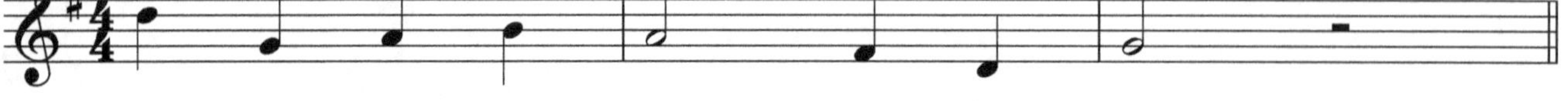

key: _____

Naming Keys

Musical Terms Word Search

```
C O M I S S I T R O F L
A D O C L E G A T O X O
M L R M R V G P O C O G
O E L S I E C O T L O M
F T Z E O S S L M X X O
F G S Z G T S C S J B N
Z O C E O R A I E Q U A
T L R F R F E C N N M I
Z D Z T U P O T C A D P
P M V A E A Y R T A I O
O T A R E D O M T O T P
X D F I N E L W G E D S
```

Give the musical terms for the following definitions. Circle them on the word seach.

1. Fairly fast, slower than allegro _____
2. Very loud _____
3. Little _____
4. Much, very _____
5. The end _____
6. Very fast _____
7. Very soft _____
8. At a moderate tempo _____
9. Soft _____
10. Moderately loud _____
11. Loud _____
12. Becoming louder _____
13. Play smoothly _____
14. Play short and detached _____

54

Naming Keys

9
Melody

Review - The Phrase

Most traditional melodies move in four measure sections called **phrases**. A phrase is a musical sentence. Like the sentence in a story, a phrase represents one musical idea. Phrases are often indicated by a long curved line called a **phrase mark**. A phrase mark looks like a large slur. This line indicates the beginning and end of the phrase.

Figure 9.1 has a phrase mark above the melody. This melody is four measures long, which is the most common length for a musical phrase.

Stable Pitches

The strongest and most **stable pitch** of any key is the tonic. A stable pitch is a note that has strength, finality, and completeness. Many melodies begin and end on the tonic. The melody in Figure 9.1 is in the key of G major and begins and ends on the tonic ($\hat{1}$).

Figure 9.1

G major

Another relatively stable pitch, is scale degree $\hat{3}$. Scale degree $\hat{3}$, is the 3rd of the tonic triad and has a certain amount of strength and stability, although it is not as strong as $\hat{1}$. The melody in Figure 9.2 ends on $\hat{3}$.

Figure 9.2

G major

55

Melody

The Unstable Pitch

Some pitches within a key are considered ***unstable***. An unstable pitch is a note that lacks finality or completeness. A composition would not end on an unstable pitch, but a phrase might. One unstable pitch is scale degree $\hat{2}$. If scale degree $\hat{1}$ is like a period at the end of a sentence, scale degree $\hat{2}$ is like a question mark. It needs an answer to complete it. The melody in Figure 9.3 ends on scale degree $\hat{2}$.

Figure 9.3

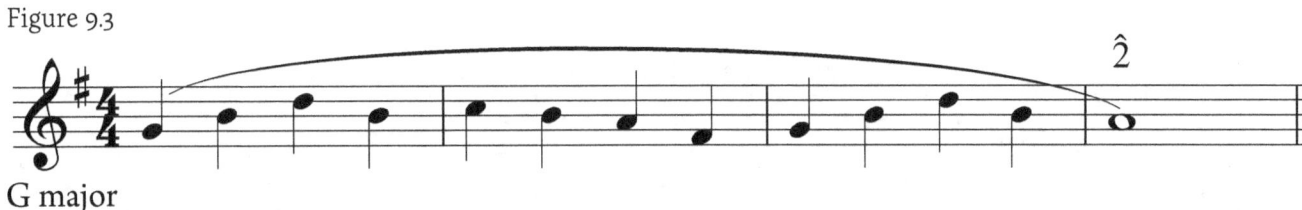

G major

1. Name the major key of each melody. Write the scale degree number for the last note and mark it as stable or unstable.

Scale degree:

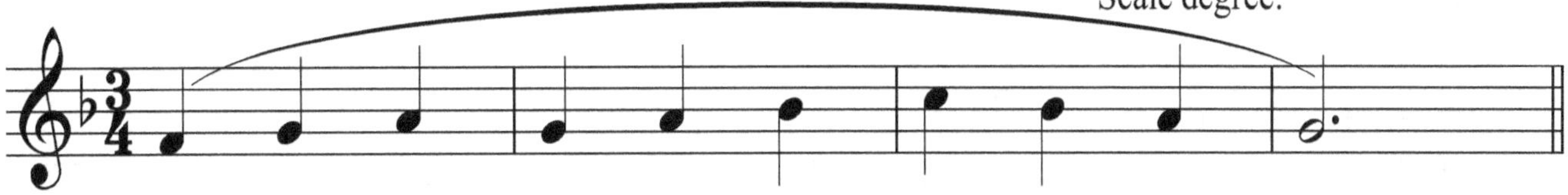

key: ____________

Scale degree:

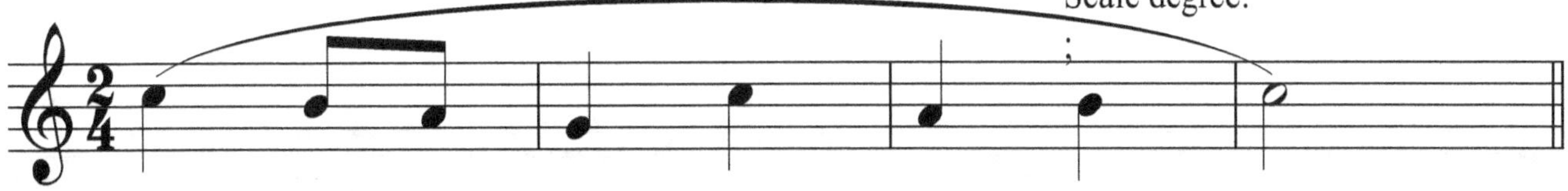

key: ____________

Scale degree:

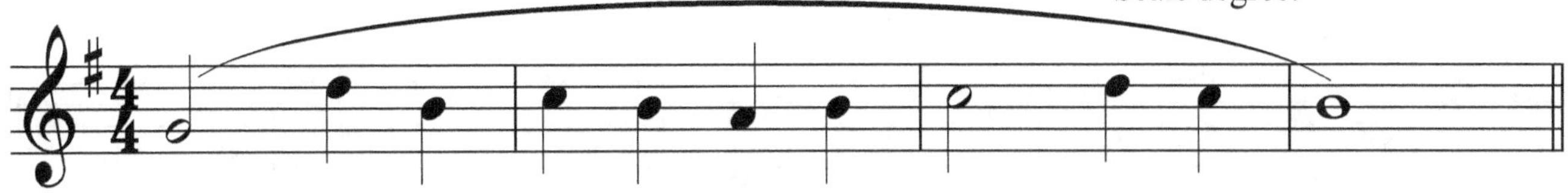

key: ____________

The Motive

Many phrases are built from smaller groups of notes called ***motives***. A motive is a specific pattern of notes and rhythms. Motives can be repeated at a higher or lower pitch. Figure 9.4 contains a melodic motive in measure one consisting of a half note, two eighths and a quarter. The notes skip up a 3rd and then step down. In the two measures that follow, the motive is repeated a step higher each time.

Figure 9.4

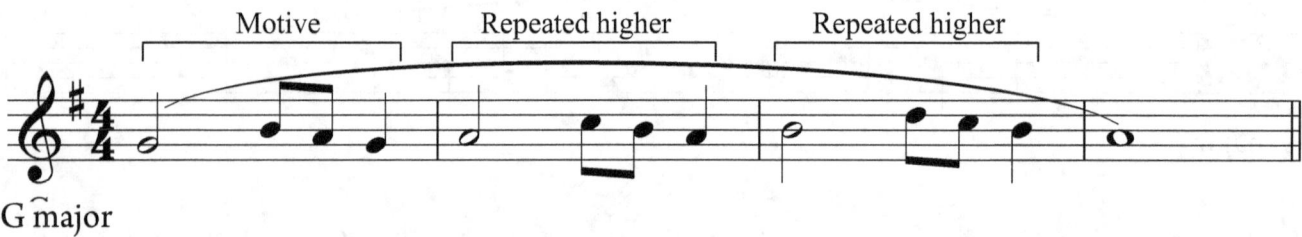

G major

1. Name the major key for each of the following melodies. Mark the phrases with slurs. Circle the melodic motives each time they occur in the melodies.

key:

key:

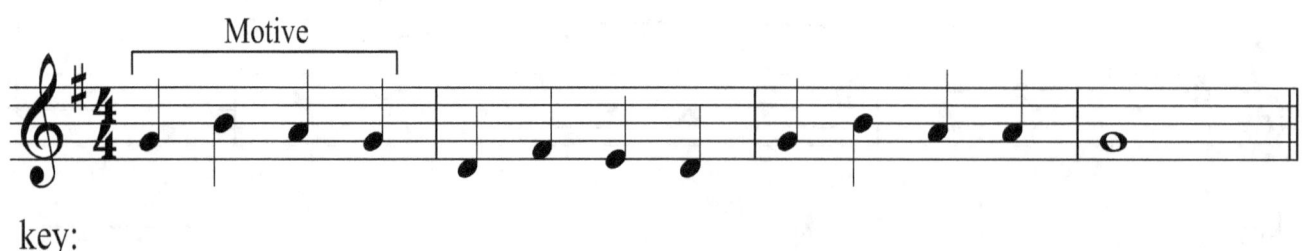

key:

Melody

Writing Melodies

In this lesson we are going to learn to write melodies that use stepwise motion and skips of a 3rd using notes of the tonic triad. Figure 9.5 is a melody in C major. The first measure contains skips of 3rds outlining the tonic triad. The rest of the melody moves in stepwise motion. The first and the final note is $\hat{1}$, which is a stable scale degree in C major.

Figure 9.5

C major

Figure 9.6 is a melody in G major. This melody uses notes of the tonic triad in G and stepwise motion. It begins on scale degree $\hat{1}$ and ends on scale degree $\hat{3}$. Both of these are considerered stable scale degrees, since they are the first and third of the tonic triad. $\hat{3}$ is less strong sounding than $\hat{1}$. Scale degree $\hat{1}$ is the best choice for a final phrase of a piece where you want a strong, final ending. Beginning and ending on the tonic helps to confirm the key.

Figure 9.6

G major

1. Complete the following melody in C major, using the given rhythm. Use stepwise motion and skips. End on a stable pitch ($\hat{1}$ or $\hat{3}$).

2. Complete the following melody in G major, using the given rhythm. Use stepwise motion and skips. End on a stable pitch ($\hat{1}$ or $\hat{3}$).

3. Complete the following melody in F major, using the given rhythm. Use stepwise motion and skips. End on a stable pitch ($\hat{1}$ or $\hat{3}$).

4. Compose a melody in F major, using the given rhythm. Use stepwise motion and skips. End on a stable pitch ($\hat{1}$ or $\hat{3}$).

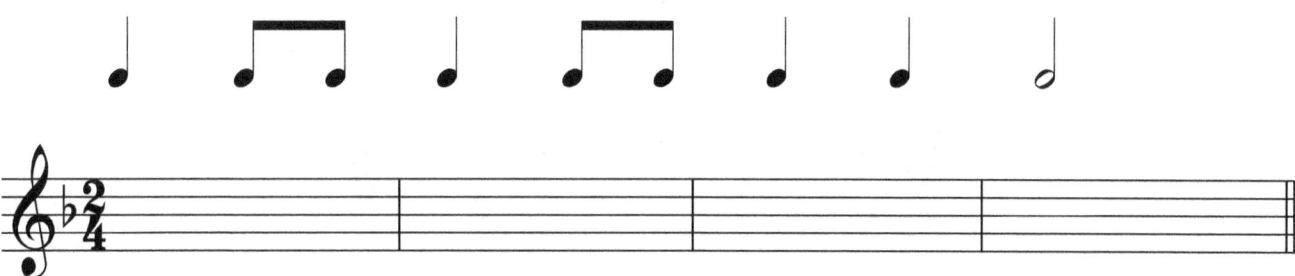

5. Compose a melody in G major, using the given rhythm. Use stepwise motion and skips. End on a stable pitch ($\hat{1}$ or $\hat{3}$).

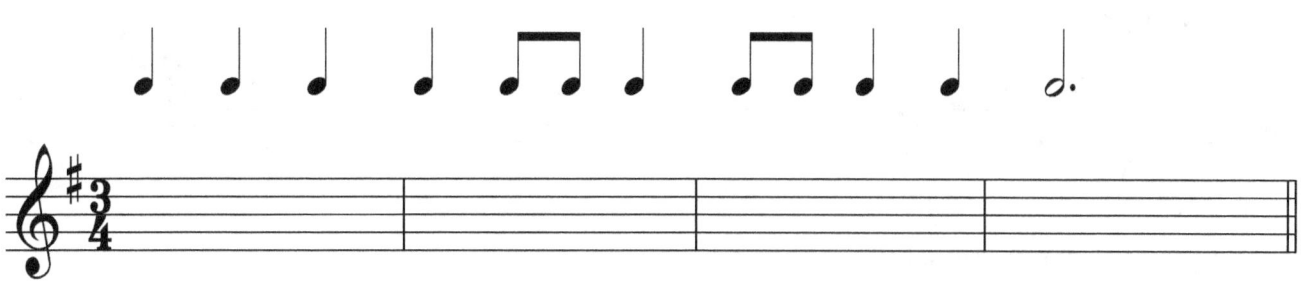

6. Compose a melody in C major, using the given rhythm. Use stepwise motion and skips. End on a stable pitch ($\hat{1}$ or $\hat{3}$).

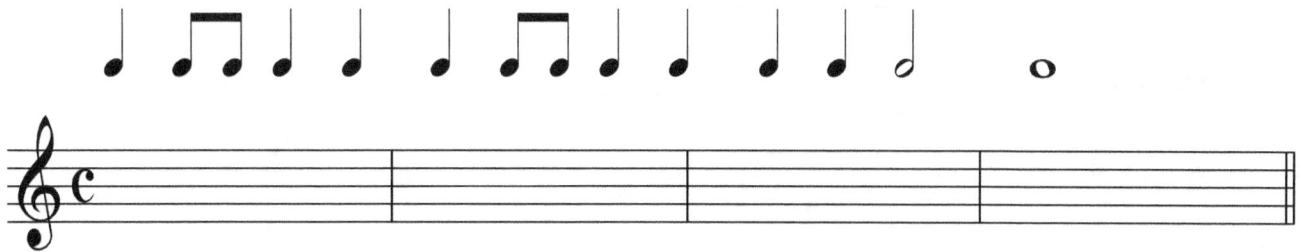

10
Music Analysis

All of the concepts we have studied in theory can be put to good use when we look at a piece of music. **Music analysis** is studying a composition and figuring out its features. In this lesson, we are going to look at music and answer questions using the information we have learned.

1. Answer questions relating to the following musical example.

a. Add the correct time signature directly on the music.

b. Name the key of this piece._____

c. Circle a complete F major scale in this piece.

d. Draw a phrase mark over the phrase.

e. On which scale degree does this phrase end?_____

f. Is this a stable degree? _____

g. Define **Allegro**._____

h. Explain the sign at letter A._____

i. Explain the sign at letter B._____

j. Label all the leading tones LT.

a. Add the correct time signature directly on the music.

b. Name the key of this piece._____

c. Circle each time motive "a" appears in this piece.

d. There are two phrases. Draw a phrase mark over each phrase.

e. On which scale degree does this phrase one end?_____

f. Is this a stable degree? _____

g. Define **Presto**._____

h. Explain the sign at letter A._____

i. Explain the sign at letter B._____

j. Name and define the sign at letter C. _____

Allegro in C

Alexander Reinagle
(1756 - 1809)

Molto allegro

a. Give the title of this piece. _____

b. Add the correct time signature directly on the music.

c. Name the key of this piece. _____

d. Name the composer of this piece. _____

e. When did he live? _____

f. There are two phrases. Draw a phrase mark over each phrase.

g. On which scale degree does phrase two end? _____

h. Is this a stable degree? _____

i. Define **Molto allegro**. _____

j. Name and define the sign at A. _____

k. Name the interval at B. _____

Review 3

1. Write the following major scales ascending and descending in whole notes using accidentals instead of a key signature. Label the Tonic (T), subdominant notes (SD), and dominant (D).

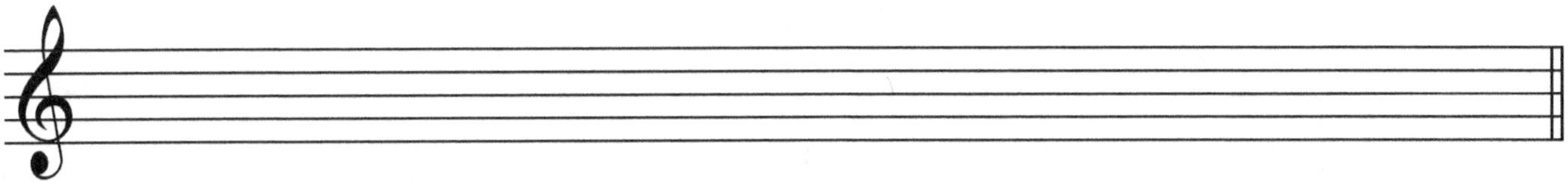

G major

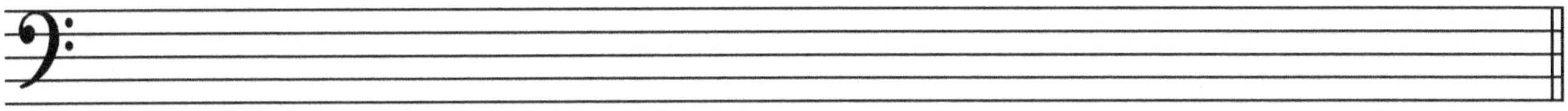

C major

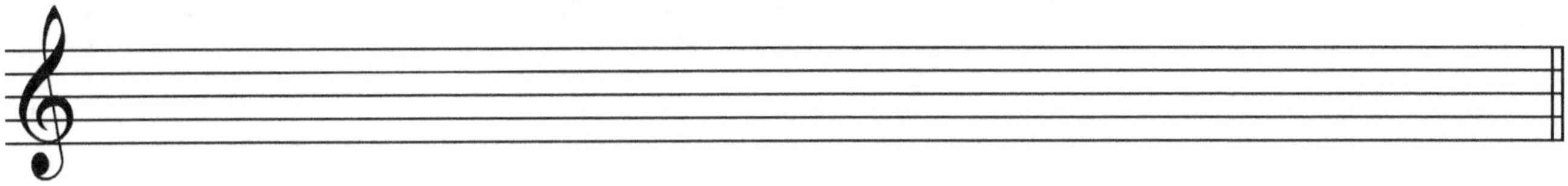

F major

2. Write the following natural minor scales ascending and descending in half notes using the correct key signatures. Label the Tonic (T), subdominant notes (SD), and dominant (D).

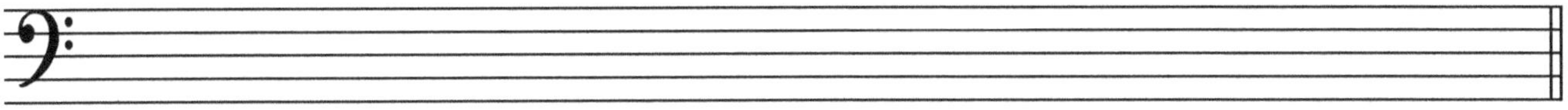

D minor

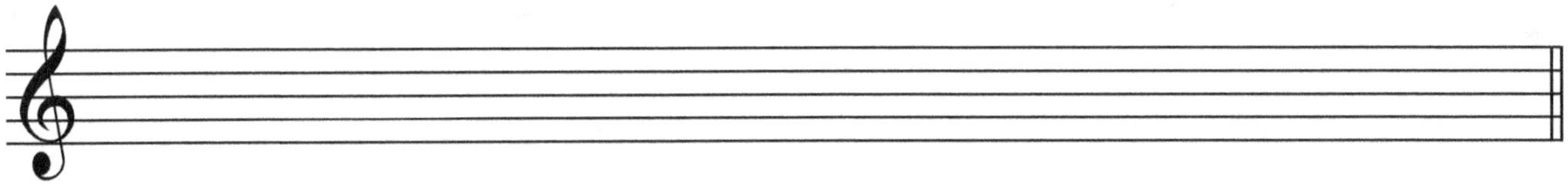

E minor

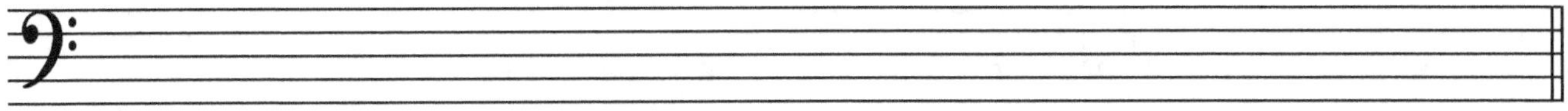

A minor

3. Add one note to complete each measure according to the time signature.

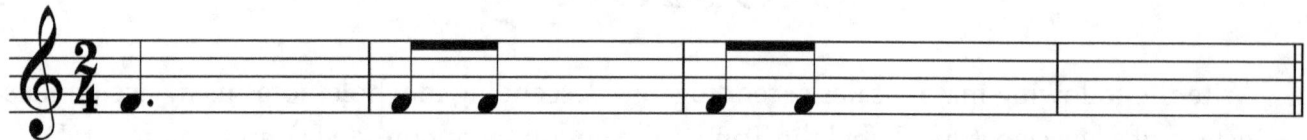

4. Add times signatures to the beginning of each line.

5. The following are all **tonic** triads. Name the key. Write the root/quality and functional chord symbol for each.

6. Compose a melody in C major, using the given rhythm. Use stepwise motion and skips. End on a stable pitch ($\hat{1}$ or $\hat{3}$).

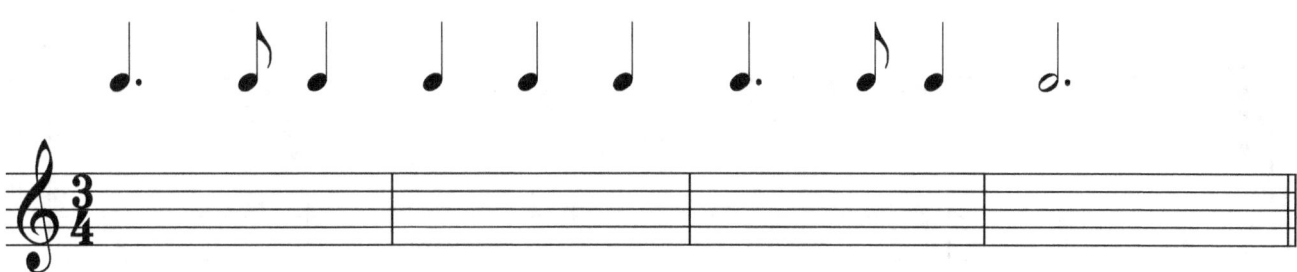

7. Match the following Italian terms with their meaning.

_____ *lento*   a. very fast

_____ *presto*   b. slowing down

_____ *rallentando, rall.* c. return to the original tempo

_____ *poco*   d. much, very

_____ *molto*   e. little

_____ *allegretto*   f. slow

_____ *a tempo*   g. fairly fast (slower than allegro)

8. Answer questions relating to the following musical example.

Study Op.125, No. 3

Anton Diabelli
(1781 - 1858)

a. Add the correct time signature directly on the music.

b. Name the key of this piece._____

c. Name the composer of this piece._____

d. Draw a phrase mark over each phrase.

e. On what scale degree does phrase one end? _____ Is this stable or unstable?_____

f. On what degree does phrase two end? _____ Is this stable or unstable?_____

g. Define **Allegretto**._____

h. Name the triad at letter A._____

i. Explain the sign at letter B._____

Music Terms and Signs

Terms

accent	a stressed note
allegretto	fairly fast, a little slower than allegro
allegro	fast
andante	moderately slow, at a walking pace
a tempo	return to the original tempo
crescendo, cresc.	becoming louder
da capo, D.C.	from the beginning
D.C. al fine	repeat from the beginning and end at *Fine*
decrescendo, decresc.	becoming softer
diminuendo, dim.	becoming softer
fine	the end
forte, f	loud
fortissimo, ff	very loud
legato	smooth
lento	slow
mezzo forte, mf	moderately loud
mezzo piano, mp	moderately soft

moderato	at a moderate tempo
molto	much, very
pianissimo, pp	very soft
piano, p	soft
poco	little
presto	very fast
rallentando, rall.	slowing down
ritardando, rit.	slowing down gradually
staccato	play short and detached
tempo	speed at which music is performed

Signs

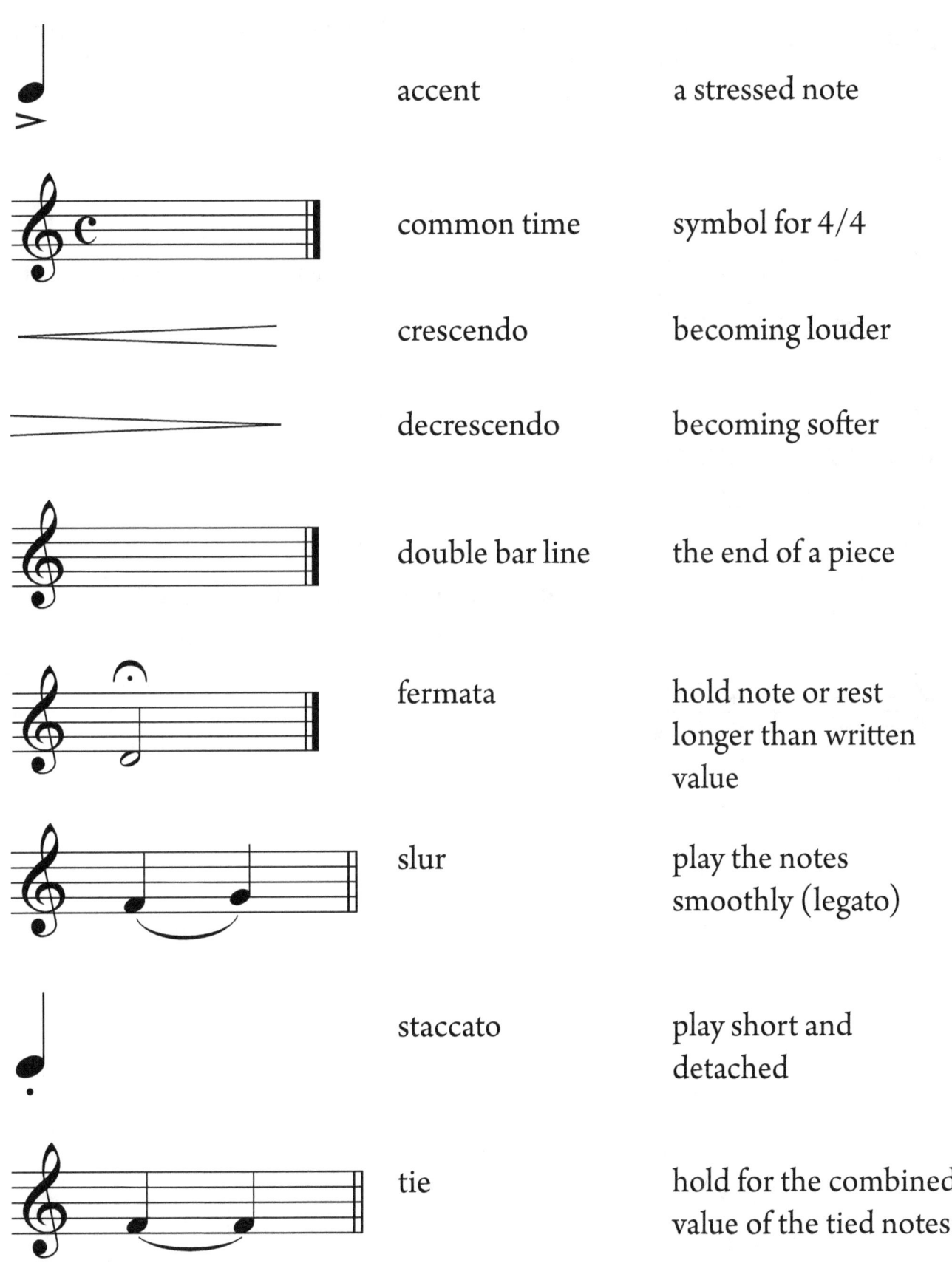

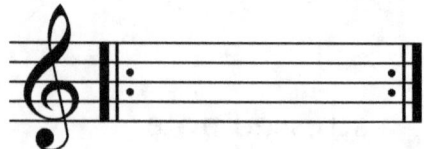

repeat marks - at the second sign go back to the first sign and repeat the music from there. The first sign is left out if the music is repeated from the beginning.

tenuto mark - when placed over or under a note, hold it for its full value.

pedal symbol - press/release the right pedal.

Terms and Signs

www.ingramcontent.com/pod-product-compliance
Lightning Source LLC
Chambersburg PA
CBHW081626100526
44590CB00021B/3624